THE ART OF GIVING

THE ART OF GIVING

By Stuart E. Jacobson

TEXT BY
DRUSILLA BEYFUS

PHOTOGRAPHY BY
STEVE LOVI

DESIGN BY
JOHN LYNCH

HARRY N. ABRAMS, INC., PUBLISHERS, NEW YORK

The many courtesies extended to the author by the staff of the Hôtel Balzac, Paris, are acknowledged with thanks.

Editor: *Ruth Eisenstein*

Excerpt on page 88, from
*The Whims of Fortune: The Memoirs
of Guy de Rothschild*, translated by
Marjorie Stoneridge. Translation
copyright © 1985 by Random House, Inc.
Reprinted by permission of the publisher.

First printing 1987

Library of Congress Cataloging-in-Publication Data

Jacobson, Stuart E.
    The art of giving.

    Includes index.
        1. Gifts—Great Britain. 2. Gifts—Europe.
    3. Celebrities—Great Britain. 4. Celebrities—Europe.
    I. Beyfus, Drusilla. II. Lovi, Steve. III. Title.
    GT3041.F7J33 1987 394 86–32229
    ISBN 0–8109–1858–7

Times Mirror Books

Printed and bound in Japan

CONTENTS

Preface and Acknowledgments

It was a source of deep satisfaction to me that my book *Only the Best: A Celebration of Gift Giving in America*, published two years ago, appealed to so many readers as a study of an interesting and important aspect of American culture.

The process of researching the book was reward enough. In my efforts to capture the creativity and imagination interwoven with love and friendship in the exchange of gifts among Americans I experienced enthusiasm, encouragement, new-found friendship, and love from the fascinating people who became the subjects of my work. I was the one who was given a great gift—a once-in-a-lifetime opportunity to cross the paths of individuals who had achieved so much and given so much.

As I traveled across America to promote the book, I was continually asked the same question, "What's next?" Without the miss of a beat I knew. I wanted to cross the Atlantic and explore the sentiments, attitudes, and experiences connected with gift giving in Britain and Europe. *Only the Best* having had enormous success in the United States, I had full confidence that my task would be as simple the second time around as the first. It wasn't. I was an unknown foreigner, and I was dealing with quite different temperaments. However, with my own sustained belief and determination and with help from many others, I managed to stay in character as the "runaway express" that Letitia Baldrige fondly likened me to in her Introduction to *Only the Best,* and I took off down the track from London to Paris to Venice.

With assistance from Earl Blackwell, editor and chairman of Celebrity Service International and editor of the *Celebrity Register,* and from *European Travel & Life* contributing editor Nancy Holmes, doors began to open: soon I was on my way to a secure feeling that the subject of gift giving evoked in Britain and Europe, as in America, a broad spectrum of memories and feelings in which love

and friendship, appreciation and gratitude, generosity and ingenuity, and even whimsy and humor have a place. In these pages, stunningly illustrated by the photographs of Steve Lovi, some very special Britons and Europeans generously share with the reader their most treasured possessions and memories.

As with my first book, *Only the Best,* I want to dedicate *The Art of Giving* to seven very special people—my "lucky seven"—whose gifts to me of enthusiasm, patience, and continued support have made this second dream of mine a reality: Ruth and Coleman Jacobson, my mother and father, who are always there for me, no matter what; Patricia Schmidt and Timothy Pearce, my invaluable assistants, whose devotion to this project and to me has deepened and strengthened our friendship; Marti Malovany, who is never too busy or too impatient with my endless requests to hold my hand; Paul Gottlieb, who in understanding and encouragement has gone far beyond just being my publisher; and Ruth Eisenstein, whom I cannot thank enough for her part in shaping this volume.

Special thanks are due to a number of people whose support of this project, and faith in it, played a major role. I gratefully acknowledge the assistance of Randolph D. Addison, William and Mary Elizabeth Boren, William D. Boren, Jr., Delphae Boyd, Nancy and Norman E. Brinker, J. Baxter Brinkmann, Brandon Burden, Charlsie Burden, Michael J. and Wynelle Collins, Douglas and Mary Covington, Anthony C. de Bruyn, John F. Eulich, Holly C. and Russell L. Farabee, Emile M. Farha, Linda V. Gray, Nancy B. Hamon, S. Roger Horchow, Patricia Zoch Johnson, Kathlene D. King, Judith Abrams Lifson, Kathy and Richard H. Luders, Carol Rae Moore, Lucille G. Murchison, Murry E. Page, Allison Browning Poage, Leon and Idelle Rabin, Ralph B. Rogers, Marilyn Rolnick, Leslie Sinclair, Diana Strauss, John M. Theirl, Linda C. Waterman, Trisha Wilson, Lois C. Wolf, Laura

Woodall, Sheila D. and A. Wayne Wright. I am indebted as well to all those who told me their stories and treated me as a friend.

Along the way a host of other people furthered the progress of this book in a host of ways, large and small. With deep appreciation I express my thanks to these individuals, on both sides of the Atlantic, who have taken an interest in *The Art of Giving:* Peter Adam, Richard Adamson, Lady Airlie, Christophe Andrew, Christophe Angevin, Alexander P. Apsis, Leonard J. Baldyga, Toula Ballas, Marie-Jeanne Baqué, Francesca Barbiari, Jack Basehart, Marzia Bava, Marie-France Bennett, Monique Berger, Stephane Birmant, Corinne Boksenbaum, John Bowes-Lyon, Beverly Bracken, Julia Bradford, Karin Brandauer, Judy Brittain, Gabrielle Buchaert, Joan Buenrostro, Cathy Cain, Carlo Canevaro, Countess Barbara Ceschi a Santa Croce, Pierre Ceyleron, Yanou Collart, Corinne Benrubi at Monsieur Renard, Theo Cowan, Peter and Beatrice Cramer, Brando Crespi, Allan Davis, Richard Day, Emmanuel Peretti Dellaroca, Julie de Matteo, Dominique Deroche, Roberto Devorik, Ariane von Dierkes, Jean Diter, Gioia Donati, Veronique Dorise, Christa Dowling, Madeline Dubois, Christian Falcucci, Jensie Farrar, Tania Farruggio, Laure de Fels, Maya Flick, Arlene Francis, Orlando Fraser, Ronald Fuhrer, John Gairdner, Virginia Gallico, Birgitte de Ganay, Michel Gardigny, Dennis Gardner, Margaret Gardner, Clare George, Lisa Gillon, Milton Goldman, Luisa Graziadei, Florence Grinda, Dr. Charles Grupper, Billy Hamilton, Jane Harker, Nicholas Haslam, Danielle Henriot-Decomis, Patricia Hipwood, Adrian Hodges, William Holbech, Olga Horstig-Primuz, Jean Howard, Thea John, Sarah Jones, Katarina Kamufo, Billy Keating, Steve Kenis, Prince Amyn Aga Khan, Ruth I. Kinnear, Wim Kramers, Jane Lahr, Evelyn Lambert, Jeffrey Lane, Sophie Langlade, George Lawson, Doris Leath, Bernard Leser, Victoria Legge-Bourke, Dominique Le Romain, Jill Lindemere, Fiona Lindsay, Michael Loeb, Sheila Logue, John Loring, Diane Lynch, Nick Maddison, Janette Mahler, Alain Mangel, Catherine Mareska, Tony Mark, Daniel Martin, Mary Martin, Ann Miller, Rosamund Monckton, Sally Morgan, Rosalina Mottini, Richard and Jane Mulkey, Angela Neville, Helen O'Hagan, Helen Ordish, Amy Penn, Claude Pianet, Alexandre Poniátowski, Juan Portela, Simon de Pury, Tonino Quinti, Ariel de Ravenel, Paul Reeves, Donald and Lois Rivkin, Antonia Rodolsi, Claude Roland, Selwa Roosevelt, Jessica Ruge, Rolf Sachs, Dr. Leonard M. Selby, Jean Sewell, Clare Sheppard, Christopher Sherville, Alexandra Shulman, Milton Shulman, Noona Smith-Peterson, Alexander Sombart, Carlos Sottomayor, Ginette Spanier, Lee Steiner, Dr. Evelyn Stern, Andrea von Stumm, Jean Tailer, Marjorie Tasby, John and Pat Kerr Tigrett, Piero Tozzoli, Filomena Tuosto, Judith L. Turner, Connie Uzzo, Elisabeth de Ribes-Van der Kemp, Claude Vogel, Conal Walsh, George Walsh, Cliff Watts, Beate Wedekind, Anne Whitehouse, Cary Woods, and Michele Wormser.

New York, February 1987   S.E.J.

ACKNOWLEDGMENTS FOR THE TEXT

In many cases my acknowledgments and Stuart Jacobson's necessarily coincide, since we have worked closely together on this book. However, I should like to make special mention of the assistance of the following—who include family, friends, and colleagues: Judy Brittain, Ruth Eisenstein, Orlando Fraser, Bernard Leser, Alexandra Shulman, Milton Shulman, Jill Spalding, and Barbara Tims.

London, February 1987   D.B.

Roland Petit
to Renée "Zizi" Jeanmarie

Roland Petit, leading French choreographer and director of the Ballet de Marseilles, and his wife, prima ballerina and film star Renée "Zizi" Jeanmarie, share a house in Marseilles and an apartment in Paris. They also share a philosophy of giving. It is based on the sudden impulse rather than the occasion, and, according to Roland, it is typically French. "Someone has an idea and says, 'Oh! I have something for you,'" is his way of describing the gift-giving process, and he can give many examples of this

kind of exchange between Zizi and himself. "We just do it like that," he says, and tells of catching sight one day, in a showcase of turn-of-the-century pieces in a jeweler's window, of a brooch in the form of an ivory rose with a diamond teardrop in the center and a jade leaf outlined in tiny diamonds. He bought it for Zizi: "I think that that rose is just a symbol of love. It's something you give, like a flower. And it's what Zizi likes the best of all the things I have given her."

THE ROMANTIC GIFT

Above, Roland Petit and Renée "Zizi" Jeanmarie

The future Empress of France, Eugénie, had only to admire a simple cloverleaf touched with dew for her suitor Louis Napoleon to present her with an emerald cloverleaf bespangled with diamonds. Such a gesture combines the essential ingredients of a truly romantic offering: a spontaneous show of the desire to please, indulgence of a whim or fancy of the beloved's, and an element of surprise.

Lovers' gifts are all meaning. Mementos symbolize intimacy, and in romantic presents it is "who" rather than "what" that counts. Classic proof is the particular attachment of the Duchess of Windsor to a charm bracelet given her by her husband, the Duke of Windsor. Of this token she said: "I love this little thing more than all the marvelous jewels our romance brought me. David added a trinket every now and then as a memento of some special occasion in our life together." Among these are a star set with a ruby, to recall a journey to Turkey, a miniature telephone, to symbolize a time when that instrument was their sole means of communication, and a tiny boat commemorating a voyage.

The Princess of Wales, too, has a collection of private jewels. Given her by the Prince of Wales, they have a more personal, informal air than the royal sparklers she dons for official engagements. Among them is a little gold pin bearing a tuft of actual tribal feathers that is a play on the classic motif of the three white feathers of the badge of the Prince of Wales.

Wooing is an inspiration to go over the top, sometimes literally. The German industrialist Gunther Sachs, during his fantastical courtship of Brigitte Bardot (he was her third husband), once flew over the rooftop of her house in a helicopter, releasing a shower of roses. Then he landed and got out carrying his little suitcase.

During his wooing of stellar model Jerry Hall, Rolling Stones leader Mick Jagger produced a birthday gesture in her honor that was a characteristic mixture of formality and pop. Texas-born Jerry describes it: "Mick gave me this huge arrangement of beautiful yellow roses rising out of a heart-shaped piece of Styrofoam." (The yellow rose has long been associated with Texas through the popularity of the 1853 song "The Yellow Rose of Texas.")

A romantic gesture right out of the past—and in fact anticipated by Proust—is recorded by Sir Cecil Beaton in his account of his sadly inconclusive affair with Greta Garbo. He tells in his autobiographical *The Wandering Years* that on the occasion of his first meeting with Garbo, in Hollywood in 1932, this most beautiful of women plucked a yellow rose from a vase with the words "A rose that lives and dies and never again returns," and that he concealed the flower in his diary, took it home, had it

Above, the Ghani villa in the Algarve

framed, and hung it above his bed. Obeying the same impulse, Swann, the ill-starred lover in Proust's *Remembrance of Things Past*, pressed to his lips the flower (in this case a chrysanthemum) that Odette had plucked from the garden and, when it withered, locked it away in a secret drawer of his desk.

A profound understanding of the loved one's personal taste in possessions undoubtedly yields gifts of evergreen charm. Indeed the recognition of what, precisely and indubitably, will please is a compliment in its own right. On a lighthearted level, this principle is implicit in a gift to Beatle John Lennon from his artist/musician wife, Yoko Ono, on his thirty-eighth birthday, in 1971: a bubble-top Wurlitzer jukebox of the kind (it played old-style 78s) found in soda fountains of the fifties. John Lennon subsequently spent many hours listening to early hits like "Dream Lover," "As Time Goes By," and Bing Crosby's "Please" (which was the basis of the Beatles' hit, "Please Please Me"). John Lennon's grand gesture to Yoko Ono bore a personal inscription that transformed a munificent gift into a very personal tribute: "This morning, a white piano for Yoko."

The present of property is almost as old as marriage and has a history in which the terms "bride price" (offered by the groom) and "dowry" (offered by the bride) play a part. Some of the circumstances surrounding the presentation of property are a great deal more romantic than others, but in any case a retreat to call one's own is a double gift, combining largesse with security. No better example is recorded than the gift that Henry II of France bestowed upon his mistress, the bewitching Diane de Poitiers in 1547—the enchanting castle of Chenonceaux in the Loire Valley. In the fifties of the present century, in a comparable romantic gesture, Baron Hans Heinrich Thyssen–Bornemisza bestowed upon his wife Nina Dyer a tiny island off Jamaica.

Nothing less than a totally new environment was the extravaganza bestowed by Amin Ghani on his wife, Nahid. A casual conversational exchange touched off the whole venture. Nahid Ghani said to British designer David Hicks, a houseguest at her Portuguese villa in the Algarve, "I don't believe you like my house." Hicks, who had previously decorated his host and hostess's apartment in London, recalls that he replied, with more honesty than tact, "You're absolutely right. I think it is dreadful."

The sequel was that Amin Ghani commissioned Hicks to create an entirely new house and garden in the neighboring terrain for him to present to Nahid. Hicks was to act as architect, interior decorator, and landscape designer, in the grand manner. An ideal site was found in the romantic vine-clad countryside overlooking the Atlantic.

Upon the completion of the new villa, Nahid Ghani, who will be spending long summer months in her elegant abode, remarked, "David has given us a jewel."

A brilliant exponent of the art of romantic giving was Edward James, eccentric English millionaire and patron of the Surrealists. He fell in love with Tilly Losch, the exquisite Viennese dancer, actress, and mime, and they were married in 1931. In what proved to be a fruitless attempt to save their tempestuous marriage, he virtually made a present to his wife of an entire ballet company; he funded during its six-month existence the brilliant company Les Ballets 1933, assembled and directed by George Balanchine, which provided many roles created specially for her. For West Dean, their house in Sussex, Edward James commissioned a carpet woven with a repeat pattern of Tilly's forever-dancing footprints.

The romantic gift on occasion finds its way into print. Liane de Pougy, the courtesan and music-hall artist who was one of the ornaments of the Parisian demimonde during the *belle époque* and the twenties, became a diarist during her later days of respectability. Her books *Mes Carnets bleues* (first published in English in 1925 as *My Blue Notebooks*) described her brief liaison with the wealthy Lord Carnarvon, whom she met at Nice when she was eighteen years old. He apparently introduced her to clay-pigeon shooting, among other diversions. To her diary she confided that he was "a delicious, agonising lover, full of charm and cruel grace. . . . I have kept a pearl in his memory, the most beautiful of all my pearls, the one valued today at a hundred thousand francs."

Love at first sight—a *coup de foudre*—was what happened the moment Laura Biagiotti—often called in America the Queen of Cashmere—cast eyes on the Castello di Marco Simone. Now her permanent residence and her company's headquarters, this castle near Rome was probably built during the first centuries of the Roman Empire. Biagiotti's partner and good friend Gianni Cigna, who bought the castle for her, realized the extent of the restorations that would be necessary, yet he was convinced by the designer's almost magical attachment to it. Thus was rescued one of the most spectacular historical sites of the Roman countryside.

Sometimes the romantic gift acquires an almost mystical significance which outlives the sentiment that prompted it. There is evidence that in the full life of Coco Chanel, the Paris dress designer who revolutionized fashion, sentiment played a paramount part. The great Russian composer Stravinsky was smitten with the young designer in Paris, in 1920, when he was working with Diaghilev. The lovers parted after two years, but Coco always kept a small remembrance of their romance: the

Fan decorated by Gustav Klimt

Laura Biagiotti's Castello di Marco Simone near Rome

little Russian icon that Stravinsky had bestowed upon her remained by her bedside until the day she died, in 1971.

Promises, promises. . . . Numberless declarations of romantic intent bite the dust of reality. Black enchantress Josephine Baker, nightclub entertainer in Paris in the twenties, numbered among her conquests the Crown Prince of Sweden; Gustav presented her with a knight on a white charger fashioned of diamonds and emeralds with a sword of pearls and a ruby eye, all in the guise of an elegant brooch. Supposedly the piece symbolized Gustav's readiness to come to her rescue, which in a sense he did; in a lean period in her generally triumphant and legendary career she had to pawn the brooch.

Even a farewell gift can be romantic, and the sweet sorrow of parting can lead to memorable last words. The fin de siècle Viennese artist Gustav Klimt marked the end of an affair by the presentation of a painted fan. One side of the pleated fan was decorated in traditional nineteenth-century style with emblems of romance. The reverse side was painted by Klimt in his own style. The painting bore the inscription (in German) "Better an ending with pain than pain without end."

The cult of courtly love did not die out with the troubadours or with the Elizabethans. It is very much alive in the household of Lord Dudley. His wife, Maureen (she was Maureen Swanson, a well-known film actress), cherishes a long love poem, "Serenade to Maureen," that he presented to her at Christmas in 1976.

Billy Dudley had intended to compose a single sonnet but found that the traditional sonnet form of fourteen lines was much too short to allow him to express all that he wanted to say. He therefore produced a sequence of six sonnets, with a literary embellishment of his own invention. "I added two lines as a kind of epilogue to each sonnet; all these extra lines put together work as a complete verse. It was a little extra conceit; the Elizabethans rather liked this kind of thing."

The "Serenade" was printed with an accompanying illustration of a woodcut depicting a swan gliding peacefully on a pastoral stream—a reference to Lady Dudley's nickname, Swan.

"When a friend asks me for a copy," says Lady Dudley, "I suspect she just wants to take it home and substitute her name for mine in the title!"

Offerings suggesting continuity of love must rate among the most appealing. The point was well made by widely admired and widely read Lady Antonia Fraser. For her "the most romantic present I ever received" was a rose hedge to plant around her house in London. Every time she goes in or out she glimpses the hedge. "It is a present daily renewed."

Lord Dudley's "Serenade to Maureen"

Tom Montague Meyer
to Fleur Cowles

Anyone who has read Fleur Cowles' books or seen her paintings knows that she is addicted to flowers. No one is more aware of this than her husband, Tom Montague Meyer, successful London entrepreneur and businessman. Naturally, on their thirtieth wedding anniversary, in 1985, Tom's thoughts turned not to jewelry, not to houses, not to horses, not to yachts, but to a way to provide more and more year-round flowers. With this in mind he designed a perfect greenhouse to be added to their older, less modern one. A two-parter, the new nursery has a larger section for controlled warm circulation and a smaller one for controlled coolness. These make it possible for Fleur to grow almost any flower (and many out-of-season ones) when she chooses.

Fleur's enthusiasm is unbounded: "Anything and everything that can improve the life of a flower has been installed inside the magical fifty-five by fifteen-foot space. Because one side faces north, Tom shielded it from the north wind by building a fifteen-foot brick wall, with attractive pillars. On these I've trained espalier morello cherries, intermingling them with roses and lacy white climbing hydrangeas. Now our sixteenth-century house is full of its needed vivid primary colors. Other plantings provide for the more sophisticated needs of our flat in a nineteenth-century Georgian house in London—the pinks, mulberries, whites, and blues that suit its high, history-laden walls."

The many friends, American and English, who enjoy the Meyers' famed hospitality, both in their flat in London and in their house in Sussex, have reason to appreciate, along with Fleur Cowles, her husband's creative horticultural gift.

Above, Fleur Cowles' greenhouse

Baron Gérard de Waldner
to Baronne Sylvia de Waldner

Brazilian-born Baronne Sylvia de Waldner is blond and beautiful, and—as she is the first to admit—always late. The de Waldners live in Paris on the Faubourg Saint Honoré.

When their seventh wedding anniversary came around ("It is very dangerous, everyone says this," acknowledges the Baroness), far from succumbing to the conventional seven-year itch, the Baron commissioned a handsome and most romantic, if pointed, gift for his charming unpunctual wife. This was a small clock set in a natural free-form piece of blue Brazilian topaz. It is designed with a diamond-studded Cupid's arrow marking the numeral seven. The tip of the arrow is a heart-shaped champagne-colored diamond. The face of the clock is mother-of-pearl, encircled in diamonds.

The theme of time stirs sentimental memories for Sylvia de Waldner: "When we met, Gérard asked me to go to a movie with him. I said, 'Give me some days to think.' Two years later we were married. . . . Then, when we made seven years, this wonderful present. It is always near me."

Baronne Sylvia de Waldner

17

*Below, Miguel Berrocal
and Princess Maria
Cristina Bragança*

The work of Spanish
sculptor Miguel Berrocal is
idiosyncratic, unusual—
even unique. So, too,
according to her account,
was Miguel's courtship, in
1972, of Princess Maria
Cristina Bragança. When
they first met, they just
exchanged addresses.
Then he began to call
every day, and one day he
came from Verona to visit
her in Rome. Lunch was
followed by a movie, the
movie by dinner, and at
dinner Miguel insisted on
giving Maria Cristina a
gold ring with a garnet.

For Maria Cristina,
"a ring is very symbolic, it
is a bond," and though she accepted it, she would not wear
it. Miguel formally asked her father for her hand in
marriage the next day, but it was a full six months before
Maria Cristina decided that the ring was "her ring, a
present from her man."

It is no ordinary ring that marked Maria Cristina's
commitment. It is actually part of an interlocking statue
called *David*, one of a series of Berrocal's mini-sculptures.
The entire edition of this work has been sold, and it amuses
Maria Cristina that she has the ring but not the sculpture.

Miguel Berrocal
to Princess
Maria Cristina Bragança

Marchese Emilio Pucci
to Marchesa Cristina Pucci

It is an understandable tendency of mothers and nannies to preserve the drawings of their little ones in the belief—or hope—that they show talent. In the case of Emilio Pucci, a childhood drawing preserved by his nanny was indeed a portent: this Florentine aristocrat grew up to become a modern Renaissance man—politician, arbiter of style and elegance, Olympic skier, founder of the fashion house of Pucci at the Palazzo Pucci in Florence, and designer whose strong prints and original textiles achieved international status from the fifties on.

Both a sentimental document and an artistic curiosity, a drawing of a cat and a dog by the five-year-old Emilio was presented by the Marchese as a special gift to his wife after their marriage, in 1959. He believes that it must be one of the first drawings that he made and signed. Painting and drawing was one of the few entertainments this strictly brought up child was permitted.

"What can be noticed in the drawing," comments Pucci's daughter, Laudomia, "is that at this very young age, as in his work later as a fashion designer, my father used imaginative colors. The animals are painted turquoise, while the details are in pink. It is probable, as he says, that even at this early age he had a feeling for two colors that he still prefers."

Marchese and Marchesa Emilio Pucci

Twiggy
to Leigh Lawson

Retaining the pert name that harks back to her first appearance on the international scene as an irresistibly appealing skinny sixteen-year-old model, Twiggy has gone on to grown-up triumphs as a full-fledged star, singing and dancing in the 1983 hit musical *My One and Only* and appearing on the English stage and in films and on television. It is an inspiriting history.

Twiggy's choice of a gift for her constant companion, British actor Leigh Lawson, delves into a different kind of history. It is a Roman antique gold ring inset with an intaglio engraving of Apollo in agate. Leigh describes the ring, which is dated circa A.D. 1080, as "beautiful, simple,

sturdy," and is intrigued that he can discern the original little hammer beats on the inside. "I am constantly reflecting on who might have worn it over the long history of its existence. And it pleases me that I would not have to take off my ring in any play that I was doing unless the action took place in a period a thousand years ago!"

The ring that Leigh presented to Twiggy is, in contrast, contemporary, though the motif is an old one. It is a specially designed love knot wrought in three colors of gold—yellow, white, and pink—and set with a diamond symbolizing a kiss. Twiggy cherishes this, "my first proper present from Leigh," and is touched by the idea behind it—the love knot.

To display these two fine and meaningful rings, Twiggy and Leigh press into service some twenties figurines given to Twiggy by Barbara Hulanicki, the dress designer who created Biba in London in the sixties.

Above, Twiggy and Leigh Lawson

Harold Pinter
to Lady Antonia Fraser

In the household of international literary notables Harold Pinter and Lady Antonia Fraser, taste turns to early-nineteenth-century jewelry, the poetry of T. S. Eliot, and strawberry-patterned china. Taking time out from the writing of critically acclaimed dramas and the directing of plays and films, Pinter has marked each special occasion—the anniversary of their first meeting, the anniversary of their wedding (in 1980), Lady Antonia's birthday—by presenting his wife with a ring. In fact, "we chose the rings together, for beauty rather than intrinsic value," Lady Antonia says admiringly of her collection of Regency paste: finely cut and polished imitation gems in some of the prettiest settings devised by early-nineteenth-century jewelers.

Both writers (Lady Antonia has to her credit a long list of esteemed and best-selling historical biographies, the latest a life of British warrior queen Boadicea, of the first century A.D.) are devotees of the work of T. S. Eliot. They have visited East Coker in Somerset, where the poet's ashes are interred. Another act of homage was Lady Antonia's choice of Eliot's poem "East Coker" from his book of verse *Four Quartets* as a gift to her husband. She presented a specially designed and bound copy of the poem—the work of Julian Rothenstein—to Pinter in Dublin during his tour as director of Simon Gray's *Close of Play*.

In lighter moments, both this man of letters and this woman of letters enjoy the triple pun—Fraser, phrase, *fraise* (strawberry)—implied in their use of Lady Antonia's favorite china.

Above, Harold Pinter and Lady Antonia Fraser

The Marquess of Tavistock to the Marchioness of Tavistock

Woburn Abbey, in Woburn, Bedfordshire, seat of the Dukes of Bedford since the mid-sixteenth century and one of Britain's stateliest houses, is the residence of the Marquess and Marchioness of Tavistock (Lord Tavistock is heir of the 13th Duke of Bedford). The banner that flies over Woburn Abbey underwent a change in 1977—a change that represented a tribute paid by Lord Tavistock to Lady Tavistock.

In that year their son and heir, Lord Andrew Howland, then fifteen years old, had been seriously injured in a car crash in the United States; in eleven months Andrew underwent nine operations. Lady Tavistock, who left Woburn to be with him during his three-month convalescence in California, tells the story of their return: "We rode up the driveway and I looked up to the top of the house. I noticed that the banner was different: it was

halved, with Robin's coat of arms on one side and mine on the other. Robin told me that this was to thank me for all that I had done. I was totally overwhelmed." Nor was the gesture intended solely as a homecoming welcome. "Robin told me that this banner will always fly over Woburn Abbey."

Lady Tavistock's mementos to her husband include seven pairs of needlepoint slippers that she has embroidered herself. Each pair is presented with a card bearing the inscription "Every stitch says 'I love you.'"

Above, Woburn Abbey, Bedfordshire

Jean Muir

Jean Muir, British dress designer noted for her purist style, declares that her collection of gifts from Harry Leuckert, to whom she has been married for some twenty-nine years, "shows total understanding of me."

Harry seems to have had this prescience from the start. Instead of the conventional wedding band he produced several little gold rings (which Jean wears on the little finger of her left hand). "They have never left my finger. I wear them in place of a wedding ring." Harry's choices give shape to her imagination. An antique Chinese casket of dark, polished wood inlaid with mother-of-pearl, probably a late-eighteenth-century container for cosmetics, when opened, reveals a number of beautifully turned small drawers and compartments and a small looking-glass on a stand. "When I look into the mirror all kinds of impressions—ghosts and spirits of the past—crowd in. The box has the character of a secret garden," says Jean.

The Leuckerts collect work by contemporary British artist/craftsmen, and have played a part in the resurgence of the whole field of the artistic crafts in Britain. The process of building up their collection provides them both

with opportunities to indulge each other. They have often turned to two artists who work in wood and whose designs have a distinctively English air for new pieces. A mutual treasure is an affectionate study of a Canadian snow goose by Guy Taplin, who works in driftwood that he picks up from the Thames; the bird stands on one leg, a wooden stick, and its head snuggles down onto the curve of its breast. As much of a favorite is a portable, rectangular piece in burr oak by Jim Partridge that can function as a container. The artist scooped out the interior, scorched the wood to darken it, and waxed the surface to a satisfyingly smooth texture.

Harry keeps a weather eye out for gifts that belong to Jean, and vice versa. Sometimes Harry will attach an occasion—such as a birthday or Valentine's Day or Christmas—to a gift, but sometimes he simply offers one out of sheer inclination.

All these varied objects have one meaning for Jean Muir. "They represent the continuing development of a relationship. They also represent the change from being young and starting out with not much money to being successful. That's quite nice."

Marisa Aumont
to Jean-Pierre Aumont

To save or not to save—it is a universal dilemma, and many a vain regret follows in the wake of lost memorabilia. Reminiscing about his early days in the theater, stage and screen actor Jean-Pierre Aumont, who starred in Cocteau's play *La Machine Infernale* in 1934 and in the stage musical *Gigi* in London in 1985, showed his wife, Marisa, a photograph of a poster by legendary poster artist Paul Colin produced in connection with the play *Famille*, in which the actor had starred in 1939 in Paris.

"It is very beautiful," said Marisa. "Whatever happened to it?"

Aumont admitted that he had not thought of it for

years, and added philosophically, "If it is gone, it is gone."

Marisa was not so philosophical, and started on a search for the poster in Paris and in other cities. Then one day in Hollywood, where she was doing a TV show, a friend made available to her his collection of possible accessories for film settings. Looking through the hundreds of random objects in the film studio's back lot, they found the very poster she had been hunting for. Thus many years after the play and many years after their conversation, Marisa was able to present her husband with this rare and, to him, priceless poster by Paul Colin for *Famille*.

Federico Fellini
to Giulietta Masina

The ornate, sometimes outrageous, fantasies of Federico
Fellini have long been the wonder of the post-war Italian
cinema. His early films—*La Strada* and *Juliet of the
Spirits*—triumphantly blended his baroque style with the
impish, coquettish quality of his wife, Giulietta Masina.
Giulietta maintains that the greatest gifts she has received
from her husband have been the roles she has played in
his pictures. These roles—in fact all the roles of his main

characters—are given tangible form in the portraits that
Fellini customarily draws in preparation for a film. (He
also designs the sets.) Giulietta particularly treasures the
drawing of herself as itinerant player Gelsomina—a role
that won her worldwide acclaim in *La Strada*, made in
1954. Other actors in that film who were sketched by
Fellini were Anthony Quinn as Zampano and Richard
Basehart as Matto.

Above, Federico Fellini and Giulietta Masina

one little fort right on the outskirts, sitting on a hill studded with trees. 'Jai' asked me if I liked it. I replied that I thought the fort the most beautiful of places. He had it restored and gave it to me."

Part of the old building, which was constructed of towers, battlements, and pinnacles, was turned into an extremely comfortable but not grandiose apartment. The round turrets became rooms: these lookouts became vantage points from which to view the princely domain of Jaipur. The Maharaja changed the name to Takht-E-I-Shai ("Seat of Kings"). The Raj Mata remembers her intense feelings of pleasure, caused as much by the delightful knowledge that the retreat was her very own as by the generosity of the deed. She reports, "We had wonderful parties at my fort."

The Raj Mata, formerly the Maharanee of Jaipur, recalls the exact moment when the idea of a most unexpected and much cherished gift took hold of her husband, the Maharaja. It was on a fine day in the early 1940s, and the then Maharaja and Maharanee of the state of Jaipur were picnicking on the borders of the capital city of Jaipur. (The Maharaja was a popular ruler and a world champion polo player. He was to be the last overlord to give up his autonomy at Independence; he died in 1970. The Maharanee was a noted beauty, the subject of many glamorous paintings and photographs.)

"We were looking at the old fortifications that guard the city: at big forts on the Delhi flank, where there used to be attacks, at small forts on the other side. There was

She is reminded of former pleasures at the apartment, where her son lives these days, by a watercolor of her fort, painted by Charles Baskerville, an American artist who had come to Nepal to paint a portrait of the King. Other pictures remind the Raj Mata of the days at the Seat of Kings. A portrait of herself in a rose-petal pink sari, seated in the London drawing room of Sir Henry "Chips" Channon, was the gift of the Danish artist, Mogens Tvede.

Most people take color for granted. It does not come into their lives dramatically; it is just always there. An exception is Anna Wintour, editor in chief of British *Vogue*, who can pinpoint her discovery of color. Before it happened, she had surrounded herself with black and white to make life simpler and more organized.

"David introduced me to color," says Anna Wintour, attributing to the influence of her husband (who is director of the chief unit of child psychiatry at the College of Physicians and Surgeons of Columbia University) her new awareness of color. She is particularly attached to a collection of modern ceramics presented to her by Dr. Shaffer. They have special significance for her because they symbolize her discovery of color and his role in it.

Dr. Shaffer adds to the collection from time to time. Many of the pieces, made in the thirties, reflect his love of the warm apricot, terra-cotta, sun-gold, and lemon tones associated with the work of the Bloomsbury painters in the twenties. Divided between their London house, where they have inspired aspects of the decor, and the editor in chief's office at *Vogue*, the ceramics proclaim in both places the gift of color.

Terry O'Neil
to Faye Dunaway

Ever since visiting a cameo workshop in Naples, many years ago, Oscar-winning American actress Faye Dunaway has been fascinated by the miniature bas-relief gems. Carved out of stone or shell, usually having layers of different colors (the figure being cut in relief on one layer, another serving as background), cameos come in many sizes, shapes, and degrees of quality. Faye became a cameo collector, but since her marriage, in 1982, to noted photographer Terry O'Neil, who also loves cameos, he has taken over. Terry always gives Faye a cameo at Christmas, and he says he "starts January the first looking for the following year." The finest cameo Faye feels she has ever seen—because of its simplicity and its size and the way the gold is wrapped around it—took Terry a year to find.

"Terry is the best present-finder there is," declares Faye. She is modest about her own talent in that area, but her gift to Terry of an oil painting of Venice, a city for which he has a deep affection, could not have been more apt.

Above, Faye Dunaway

Desmond Park
to Dame Kiri Te Kanawa

As a child, Kiri Te Kanawa, the brilliant soprano from New Zealand, named Dame Commander of the British Empire in 1982, acquired a love of butterflies in the open spaces of her native land. This explains her special feeling for a butterfly painting commissioned by her husband, Desmond Park, as a birthday present, about 1976. The work of Raymond Ching, a British artist known for his realistic nature studies, the watercolor depicts a single butterfly. Dame Kiri feels an affinity for the subject of the painting: "The butterfly is shown as if trying to escape from the surface or attempting to fly out of the picture. It is symbolic of my character."

Above, Dame Kiri Te Kanawa

35

Oscar Lerman
to Jackie Collins

Jackie Collins has a new and different best-seller at the top of the list about every season, but when it comes to cars there is a notable constant in her life—her silver fastback Mustang. The much-traveled car is called Mustang Sally after the famous song by the soul singer Wilson Pickett. Her husband gave it to her in America as a wedding present in 1966, and she took it back with her to England, where it was the object of much admiration because they didn't have the fastback Mustang there. "I kept it in London all those years and I never wanted to part with it because I loved it so much and it had such a sentimental value to me. . . . When I came to live in America permanently five years ago, I thought I cannot be without my Mustang, so I brought it back to America." Completely restored, it is a collector's item, but more important, "the car has a lot of great memories." One of them is of driving to the South of France with Oscar and their three little girls, and all their luggage in what is "not the biggest car in the world." Another is of taking a wrong turn (with Oscar driving) and ending up in the middle of the desert on their wedding night. "So I never allowed him to drive it after that," reports Jackie. As the co-owner of the private clubs named Tramp, one on Jermyn Street in London and one in the Beverly Center in Los Angeles, Oscar Lerman is fully occupied without driving Mustang Sally.

Ettore Sottsass
to Barbara Radice

A collection of drawings that Ettore Sottsass made for Barbara Radice includes one of an owl. "The little bird's face has a decidedly scared expression," Barbara notes, and she explains that it is due to "all the challenging notions in the air."

The "air" referred to is the ambience of Memphis, a Milan firm—and also a movement, a school, and a philosophy—of which Ettore Sottsass is the intellectual leader and founder and Barbara Radice, a writer on design, is art director. Interested in the continuous updating of contemporary figurative culture, the international designers and architects of the Memphis group follow an aesthetic—pioneered by Sottsass as early as the sixties—that rejects functionalism and holds that design should be used to communicate.

Like Memphis designs, the collection of drawings drawn for Barbara by her close companion of over a decade succeed in communicating in a highly individual and idiosyncratic way. Among the sketches is one done when Barbara had a bad cold. Ettore personified the bug, saying it was "like the picture of a dragon, intended to ward off evil spirits, on a Chinese book."

Both designer and art director treasure the collection as reminders of moments in their years of companionship and of days when there were fewer business dinners to attend and more time to make drawings.

Gianni Bulgari
to Nicole Bulgari

The endearing Italian word *micio* (kitten), applied by
Gianni Bulgari to Nicole Bulgari in the days when their
love story began, inspired her cat-emblem signature—and
much more.

Nicole fills in: "*Micio* is a sign of tenderness; a kitten
is something soft, lovable. Because he called me *micio*,
I signed my letters with a cat when we used to write to
each other—whatever I used to send, sometimes a
postcard with just that cat signature."

Over the years Gianni Bulgari, whose elegant and
original designs for jewelry have captured the imagination
of the haut monde, has created for Nicole many unique
pieces that transfer from paper to precious metals her
micio signature. Brooches, pendants, and even a traveling
photograph holder for her handbag take off from her
kitten motif.

Peter Viertel
to Deborah Kerr

"My most precious gift is on my wrist. I wear it all the
time and will never take it off," says actress Deborah Kerr
of the bracelet of silver and gold chain links given her by
husband Peter Viertel on their twenty-fifth wedding
anniversary, July 23, 1985. Deborah also wears on this
hand a wedding band with ruby hearts and diamonds
designed by Peter and made by the local jeweler in the
Swiss village of Klosters, where they live.

The couple first met on the set of the film *The
Journey*, made in 1958 amid the baroque glories of the city
of Vienna. Deborah was starring, with Yul Brynner, and
director Anatole Litvak had called in his friend the
novelist Peter Viertel (known also for having written the
scripts for the film versions of Hemingway's *The Sun
Also Rises* and *The Old Man and the Sea*) to assist with the
dialogue.

Peter's remembering this anniversary somehow took
Deborah by surprise. She recalls that in his typical shy
way Peter said, "I think it's our anniversary, isn't it?" and
handed her the little box containing the bracelet. She
marked the occasion by giving Peter a classic Scottish
silver bowl inscribed with a P on one handle and a D on
the other, and just the right size to hold Peter's favorite
health-giving sunflower seeds. Deborah reflects, "Twenty-
five years is a sort of halfway house; you might not make
it to the thirty-fifth or forty-fifth, so the twenty-fifth is
very important."

Peter Viertel and Deborah Kerr

Charlotte Rampling
to Jean-Michel Jarre

A fascinating contrast is offered by an exchange of presents between Charlotte Rampling, the noted British beauty and film actress, and her husband, Jean-Michel Jarre, the French composer of electronic music.

The actress presented her husband with an illuminated bust of Beethoven carved out of a single block of glass by the French sculptor Lucien Lafaye (1896–1975), one of a limited edition of three. Acquiring this extraordinary piece had taken years of effort. The couple had first admired it in the famous lighting atelier of Jean Perzel but it was not for sale. It was still not for sale when Perzel's nephew took over the shop. But because Jean-Michel adores Beethoven, Charlotte was determined

to have it and finally persuaded the dealer to part with the bust. Presented with the piece at Christmas in 1981 Jean-Michel was totally overwhelmed and delighted.

Equally apt, although very different, is the chimpanzee doll that Jean-Michel gave Charlotte as a remembrance of her enchanting performance in the film *Max Mon Amour*, a black comedy about a woman who falls in love with a chimp and brings it home to live with her husband and child. "I sometimes miss the people I act with, and Jean-Michel thought this was one leading man that I could actually bring home and keep!"

Charlotte owns another monkey doll, named Big Boss, presented to her by the film's crew.

Above, Jean-Michel Jarre and Charlotte Rampling

Carlo Ponti, Jr., and Edoardo Ponti
to Sophia Loren

The striking beauty and dramatic ability of Sophia Loren have won her triumphs and successes beyond counting—as well as the adoration of a worldwide audience. But Loren singles out as one of the grandest moments of her life the experience of first hearing the heartbeat of her unborn child.

None of Loren's many achievements, including the winning of the Oscar for *Two Women* in 1961, have given this brilliant actress—and her husband, Carlo Ponti, the celebrated film producer—the joy that her achievement of bringing to term their two children has brought them. Indeed the whole Italian nation, it seems, having suffered

THE GIFT TO A CHILD

through the disappointment of two previous miscarriages, rejoiced in the births of Carlo, Jr., and Edoardo.

The extensive traveling that Sophia Loren's varied roles require has meant frequent interruptions of a relationship with her sons that is understandably very loving and close. Facing one of these separations, young Carlo, then aged three, had the idea of giving his mother, as he said, "something that will always remind you of me." He covered his hand with bright paint and made an imprint on a piece of paper. Edoardo, when he reached the age of three, followed suit. These bright little handprints in their frames accompany Sophia Loren wherever she goes.

Children begin to receive presents long before they have even a glimmer of the concept of gift giving. The silver rattle, the furry teddy bear, the cuddly rag doll are merely facets of the new environment they enter when they are born. The awareness that gifts come from people is a realization that occurs at different times to different children.

Surprisingly little light is shed on the subject by autobiographical literature, though such memories are surely stored in many adult minds. One early gift lingers in the memory of Italian superstar Sophia Loren. She has told about a present given to her when she was five years old by her father, when she met him for the first time. Her parents lived apart, and he came back to the village of Pozzuoli to visit the family. He had brought with him "a blue pedal cart, fashioned after one of the Italian roadsters. . . . I had never seen anything like it." Painted on the automobile was her nickname, Lella. Years later the actress visited her aunt and uncle, who were still living in the old flat, and she asked what had happened to the little car. Her uncle clambered up to a hidden recess and brought down "the little blue car, cobwebby and faded, an old wasps' nest under the steering wheel." Placed on the floor, it rolled easily toward the door. "'It's silly to keep the little car,' I said, but I did not tell my uncle to throw it away."

Sir Yehudi Menuhin, one of this century's leading violinists, remembers his three-year-old self being given a present by one of his father's teachers, the Superintendent of Hebrew Schools in San Francisco, where the Menuhins lived. Even at this tender age Yehudi passionately wanted a violin. The Superintendent, aware of his longing, gave the boy a toy instrument made of metal. The maestro recalls, "It was very badly received. I went into a rage and stamped on it. Already I knew that this was not a real violin." Little did Yehudi know that there was a true benefactor waiting in the wings, and that at the age of twelve he would be given not merely a real violin but a Stradivarius.

Not only the gift but the giver of the gift is recalled in a childhood reminiscence by versatile stage and screen star and author Dirk Bogarde. He relates that when he was a child, an artist's model known to him as Aunt Kitty lodged with the family. The "dazzling eyes, the hennaed hair frizzled about the pale oval face, the coarse laughter are still, after so many years, before me and remain indelibly a part of my life." Aunt Kitty danced to records on a gramophone, loved beautiful fabrics, and awoke in the young boy a sense of beauty and drama. She would return from unexplained absences bearing amazing gifts for the family, including "a basket of shells of all kinds and

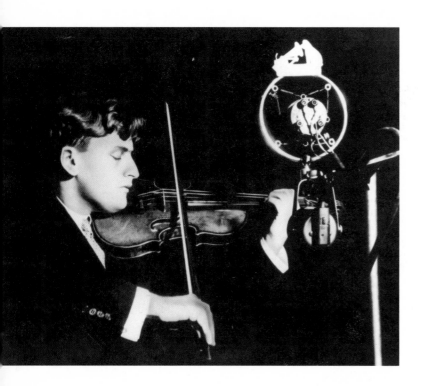

Yehudi Menuhin

shapes for me." One day Aunt Kitty vanished. She had gone off, quite willingly, with a rich sultan from the East Indies, leaving all her possessions behind, and leaving Dirk with his shells and his memories.

A present of a bouquet of yellow roses to a stagestruck young boy called Alec Guinness has never been forgotten. As a child Alec was taken to the theater to see the music-hall comedienne Nellie Wallace and was so enraptured that he spent some of his precious pocket money on a bouquet for her, which was delivered by his adult companion. Immediately afterward, possibly because of his feverish excitement, he succumbed to an illness that lasted for some months. After he had been in bed for a week, Nellie Wallace sent him a bouquet of yellow roses with a get-well note. (His adult companion had gone to the theater, explained the circumstances, and asked Miss Wallace to send Alec a postcard.) Sir Alec recalls the incident in detail: "I can remember protesting loudly when the water was changed in the vase; I was under the impression that Nellie had provided not only the roses but the vase and water as well."

Dressing up is one of the most enjoyable games of childhood—a game that perhaps we never really outgrow. Children can do their imagining with the aid of just a garment or two and a stick of makeup, but given half a chance they relish the opportunity to don authentic costumes accurate to the last fastening. To be able to wear historical costumes made by leading designers was the lucky break that came the way of the children of Jack Hawkins and his wife, Dorene Laurence, when the noted British character actor was playing a leading role, that of Quintus Arrius, in the epic movie *Ben-Hur*, directed by William Wyler, in 1959. The costume designer, Liz Haffenden, and her assistant presented replicas of the garments worn in the movie to the three Hawkins offspring—Nicholas, aged nine, Andrew, aged eight, and Caroline, aged four—as well as two other youngsters, David Wyler, aged eight, son of the director, and Fraser Heston, son of Charlton Heston (who played the hero, Judah Ben-Hur). Dorene relates that the designers made a special effort to include her very young daughter: "They made her a proper silken robe of the kind worn by Roman ladies, with a little pearly crown. They even gave her a false hairpiece so that she could wear her hair in the authentic fashion of the times." The delight that the youngsters took in their costumes was hardly paralleled by the reaction of Jack Hawkins to his. As his wife notes, "Jack had to wear a full armor-plated outfit. . . . The poor man was virtually in a tin can. In the Roman heat of August he lost pounds and pounds of weight."

Among the best presents that a parent can give a

Andrew, Caroline, and Nicholas Hawkins in Ben-Hur *costumes*

Paul Bocuse using his Opinel knife

Salvatore Ferragamo with Leonardo

Salvatore Ferragamo with Leonardo

Bilston enamel box by Halcyon Days with themes from compositions by George Benjamin

child is one that indicates faith in the offspring's talent or ability. At the age of six, Paul Bocuse, the chef who is regarded as ambassador-at-large for French cuisine, was given a present expressing that kind of faith by his father, George Bocuse, himself a well-known chef. Paul is the inheritor of a family tradition that began in the mid-eighteenth century and that has flowered in the distinguished establishment run under his name in Collonges-au-Mont d'Or, near Lyons, which earned its third *Michelin Guide* star in 1965. The knife that the six-year-old Paul received was an Opinel with a sharp blade, the kind many French country children carry around with them for whittling and making wooden whistles. It became a talisman for young Paul, who—it must be said in the talisman's favor—was able successfully to prepare dishes such as veal kidneys in Madeira sauce at the age of eight. Paul kept the knife with him during military service in World War II. In peacetime he likes to use it, for luck, in trying out new recipes, and the knife invariably accompanies him to the many grand dinners he has to attend. Although he collects knives of many different types and sizes, this is the one that Bocuse keeps on hand at all times and the one whose cutting edge is always kept sharp.

The validity of rewards in the raising of children is argued pro and con. A positive view is taken by Leonardo Ferragamo of the famous Italian shoe firm. He rates as his most precious gift from his father, Salvatore Ferragamo, the founder of the firm, a reward he received when he was six years old: because Leonardo had received top marks in school, he was allowed into the cobblers' workrooms, where he was taught to do small tasks. He recollects learning to wax the thread used for hand stitching leather and gathering up bent nails and hammering them into shape for re-use. "I was taught the first rules of shoemaking in the same way as my father learned the craft at the cobbler's knee when *he* was a boy." Looking back at this experience of 1959, Leonardo Ferragamo realizes, and observes gratefully, "One of my father's abilities was to motivate people."

A childhood memory is kept alive for H.R.H. Princess Chantal of France by a wedding present. When she was about twelve years old and her family was living in Portugal, she recalls that Haile Selassie, Emperor of Ethiopia, paid a state visit to that country. Like many others, she was greatly impressed by his extraordinary presence, and was moved to read a great deal about him and his country. Years later the Emperor was privately received by her father in their château in France, and the Princess, then engaged to marry Baron François de Sambucy, told Haile Selassie of her girlish admiration for him. Charmed, the Emperor promised to send her a wedding present. In due course it came through the diplomatic mail—a most beautiful gold bracelet bearing the Emperor's coat of arms, with the inside threaded in elephant hair—and the Princess "loved it from that day forth."

Achievement on the part of offspring is a most satisfying incentive for gift giving. Such an occasion was afforded his parents by George Benjamin, one of Britain's youngest and most promising composers—the youngest composer ever to have a work performed at a Promenade Concert in the Royal Albert Hall. The Benjamins, who own the London shop Halcyon Days, which specializes in Bilston enamel boxes (ready-made and custom-made), were able to mark this event (1980), together with George's twenty-first birthday (1981), by presenting him with an enamel box inscribed not only with loving birthday wishes but also with bars of music from the composition that was played at the Prom concert, titled "The Ring by the Flat Horizon."

Remembrances bestowed by grown children on parents often reach far back. A particularly engaging way of expressing family solidarity was found by the three sons of the first Lord Astor of Hever. After Lord Astor had left England to live in France, in 1962, they presented him with a solid-silver replica in miniature of Hever Castle, the Astor country seat at Edenbridge, Kent. The historic castle, now open to the public, was given by Henry VIII to Anne of Cleves following their divorce. The model, made by crown jeweler Garrard, is 5½ inches square and 3½ inches high and includes the moat surrounding the castle. Inscribed "Hever Castle/Lord Astor of Hever/from his three sons/Gavin Hugh and John/Christmas 1963," the silver miniature Hever Castle was bequeathed to the owner's grandson Johnny (son of Gavin), the third Lord Astor.

Children interested in mementos can count on the responsiveness of the great and famous. At the age of twelve Princess Elizabeth of Yugoslavia was already a keen autograph hunter. With her family she was living in the same hotel in Montreux, Switzerland, as the composer and conductor Richard Strauss. She remembers plucking up her courage after one of his concerts and asking him for an autograph. To her surprise and delight, Strauss gave her a photograph of himself conducting, signed and dated and inscribed to her. To the Princess Elizabeth the photograph recalls not only the great man but also the amusing anecdotes about him that circulated in Montreux. According to one of these reports, Strauss was so dedicated to his art that he would take the score he was working on to bed with him every night and his wife

View of Hever Castle, Edenbridge, Kent

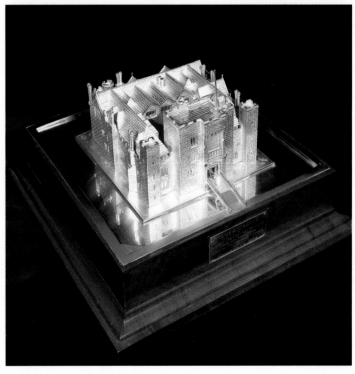

Miniature silver replica of Hever Castle

Marie Helvin

would have to take it away to get him to stop working and go to sleep.

Presents exchanged by adults that pick up on childhood emotions and interests can combine many levels of feeling. An instance is supplied by fashion model and international charmer Marie Helvin, formerly married to British photographer David Bailey. As a child growing up in Hawaii, Marie became fascinated by the necklaces of flowers that are an emblem of Polynesia, and during her years in Europe she retained her love for these leis. In 1984, when British pop artist Brian Clarke was ending a visit to her during a stay in Honolulu, she made him, as a farewell memento, a lei of fragrant frangipani from the back garden. Clarke, who is collected by, among others, ex-Beatle Paul McCartney and who created a number of designs for Beatles record sleeves, pressed the flowers, and when he returned to Britain used the lei in a collage that also incorporated sheets from a Honolulu newspaper published during his visit. Exhibited at his show in London, the collage was bought by Marie's good friend Mark Shand, who presented it to her, prompting her to make the comment "I feel as if I am part of the painting."

First presents to a baby are often given with the future in mind. Such was certainly the case when Tina Lutz produced a lighthearted offering for the first-born of her friend David Bailey and his wife, the classic English beauty Catherine Dyer. Tina, whose own rare loveliness is widely hymned in print, is the Japano-German wife of international restaurateur Michael Chow, the eponymous Mr. Chow. She set baby Paloma Bailey, born in 1985, on a predestined path of chic by giving her a little Chanel handbag.

A child who earned his present was Lucas, son of conductor André Previn. Introduced by his father to the London Philharmonic Orchestra at the age of eighteen months, the little boy did not dissolve into tears but looked around with great interest at the smiling faces, and, when handed his papa's baton, waved it with panache. Subsequently, members of the orchestra presented Lucas with his own baton, half the size of his father's, framed and with an engraved plaque commemorating his debut. The trophy hangs in André Previn's study at his home in London, where father and son spend many hours listening to their favorite music.

Any discussion of childhood and presents should include the category of gifts from the father to the mother in honor of the arrival of the newborn. Often these remembrances take the form of jewelry or some other long-lasting keepsake.

A playful variation on the theme was devised by

Roland Penrose, Surrealist painter, connoisseur, and collector, who was knighted in 1966 for his services to the arts. On the birth of their son, Antony, in 1947, Penrose gave his wife, Lee Miller, an ebony necklace with a medallion which he overpainted with a caricature of a cat looking quizzically out of its frame. Lee Miller, beautiful model, photographer, war correspondent, and the muse of many artists, had a penchant for such odd, unconventional jewelry. "She would often live in a piece picked up in a dime store while her Cartier jewelry languished in a drawer," Antony said of his talented mother, whose photographs appeared in *Vogue* magazine for over three decades.

One of the unchanging aspects of giving presents to small children is the unpredictability of their reactions. A five-year-old boy taken to the circus by Milton Shulman, drama critic of the *London Standard*, was asked after the performance which part of the show he had enjoyed most. The clowns? The acrobats? The elephants? The jugglers? The young theatergoer did not hesitate. "It was all that room under the seats," he answered cheerfully. This comment turned out to be a serviceable present to the drama critic.

The element of surprise, of mystery, even of secrecy, that plays a part in playthings addressed to the young can also have its place in mementos given by grown offspring to a parent. Lady Antonia Fraser, noted author of biographies and thrillers, found an enchanting way of commemorating the sixtieth birthday of her mother, the Countess of Longford, a distinguished writer of historical biography, mother of eight children, and wife of the Earl of Longford, a former leader of the House of Lords. Lady Antonia commissioned from William Phipps, a well-known British silversmith, a silver egg inscribed formally with her own and her mother's initials and the date, August 1966. The egg opened to reveal a smaller silver egg engraved in the giver's handwriting "Love from Antonia," with three kisses.

There is a famous incident about a gift to Albert Einstein in his early childhood. When he was five years old, and ill in bed, his father gave him—or perhaps showed him—a pocket compass, and Albert was impressed by the fact that no matter which way the compass was turned, the iron needle always pointed in the same direction. In later life the archetypal scientist himself was cautious about associating the compass with his development into a physicist, but to lay people the connection between the compass and the Nobel prize–winning theories seems irrefutable. And the image of the young mind first becoming aware of the forces in space is irresistibly appealing.

Ebony necklace with cat medallion

49

Dame Margot Fonteyn
to Carla Fracci

The Italian prima ballerina Carla Fracci came into the
world of the ballet reluctantly and might never have really
become part of it had it not been for the inspiration
provided by the legendary British ballerina Dame Margot
Fonteyn.

"I had always been in the country with my
grandmother, so the first year as a student in Milan I was
not happy. I found the work very heavy. It was difficult.
I found myself in a world I did not know; I did not
understand what it was to be a dancer."

Then Dame Margot came to La Scala with the
Sadler's Wells ballet and danced Aurora in the three-act
narrative ballet *The Sleeping Beauty*. "I was a student, a
little girl no more than twelve. Watching her, for the first
time I understood what it meant to dance. I watched very
carefully this most beautiful dancer. From then I started
to work very hard. . . . The idea of the theater, what it
meant to be a dancer, to be onstage, to give so much . . .
it was fantastic."

Little girl that she was, after the performance instead
of requesting the traditional autograph Carla impulsively
asked, "If you have a tutu that you don't use anymore, can
I have it?"

"And she gave it to me!" Carla is still thrilled by the
recollection. Since then the two dancers have worked
together many times and have often talked of the tutu.
"And," Carla adds, "Margot knows, because I always talk
about it, that she was my first inspiration."

*Above, Margot Fonteyn, Rudolf Nureyev,
and Carla Fracci taking a curtain
call after* Romeo and Juliet

Sir John Mills and Lady Mary Mills with their children, Hayley, Jonathan, and Juliet

Juliet, Hayley, and Jonathan Mills
to Sir John Mills
and Lady Mary Mills

The memorabilia accumulated over the years by actor and director Sir John Mills and his playwright wife (whose pen name is Mary Hayley Bell) are many and glamorous. But they cherish most—and regard as a precious gift—the letters written to them by their children, Juliet, Hayley, and Jonathan. Lady Mills reads from them tenderly and with a touch of sadness, because "they've all grown up and flown away."

"Listen to this one from Juliet after she had written and produced her own play, called *A Red Sky*: 'My darlings, it was all for you, everything I ever do is all for you. I wish you'd seen it . . . you would have liked the funny bits. Because you like being funny, don't ya. I love you.' And this one from 'Bags' [Hayley's nickname]: 'Dear Mummy, Nanny has been beastly. You did say we could eat our sausages with our fingers, well, Nanny said, in a sneezy voice, that we could not, with *her*.' And Jonathan wrote: 'Dear Mum and Daddy, This morning we had chapel. I will tell you about one of the prettiest sights I've ever seen. The priest leaning at the altar with a long gold robe on, two of the choir kneeling at the altar.'"

The charm of the letters is that each expresses the passing truth of a moment. Together they are a testament to years of constant love in a growing family, and they keep cherished memories from fading.

Elsa Schiaparelli
to Marisa Berenson

Schiaparelli, the wittiest and one of the most innovative couturieres to enchant Paris in the thirties, could have chosen no more engaging model than her granddaughter Marisa Berenson, beauty, socialite, stage and screen star.

On a summer's evening Marisa often wears a Schiaparelli jacket that was a gift from her grandmother. Made of fine, light-weight linen embroidered in black and white flowers, the jacket, which in other hands would be a collector's item, is among several designs given Marisa by Schiaparelli. The thought of allowing her Schiaparellis to become museum pieces does not occur to her. Sometimes Marisa wears the jacket with a sequined skirt (also a gift from her grandmother), at other times with pants. Whatever the sartorial combination may be, the jacket keeps fresh the memory of her grandmother's creativity: "I always wear Schiaparelli in Schiaparelli's honor."

Their Serene Highnesses
Prince Albert, Princess Caroline,
and Princess Stephanie
to His Serene Highness
Prince Rainier III of Monaco

The expressiveness of the human hand has inspired artists through the ages, from as far back as prehistoric cave paintings. It is a motif important in art both Western and Eastern, both folkloristic and sophisticated.

This theme occurred to the three children of His Serene Highness Prince Rainier when, in 1983, they were pondering their Christmas gift to him. The fact that Prince Rainier is a collector of bronzes steered them toward the idea of a sculpture, and after due deliberation they decided on a portrayal of their hands as a subject

that would please him. Having agreed upon this, they commissioned the internationally known Dutch sculptor Kees Verkade (whose bronze portrait head of the late Princess Grace of Monaco is in the National Portrait Gallery, Washington, D.C.) to carry out the work; it was he who determined the positioning of the hands. The sittings had to be conducted in the greatest secrecy in order to keep the present a complete surprise to the Prince. The work was cast by the foundry Venturi Arti in Bologna, Italy—a final step that was also handled successfully by the young royal conspirators.

Above, The princely family of Monaco

His Royal Highness Prince Talal
to Her Royal Highness Princess Firyal of Jordan

Princess Firyal
of Jordan with her son
Prince Talal

For Princess Firyal, sister-in-law of King Hussein of Jordan, there is one gift of little intrinsic value that is to her a treasure beyond price.

At the age of seventeen, her son Prince Talal sustained in a waterskiing accident injuries so severe that doctors doubted whether he could make a complete recovery. A year of medical treatment and hospitalization in the United States followed, during which time, as the Princess puts it, "he fought like a hero for survival." On being discharged from the hospital, Talal was able to join the Jordanian army's Special Forces Unit, to train for his army commission at Britain's Royal Military College,

in Sandhurst. The army awoke in him a passion for parachuting, and he was determined to win his wings. After being graduated from Sandhurst in 1983, he continued to train as a parachutist with the Special Forces Unit and completed his forty jumps.

At Christmas 1985, the Princess received from her soldier son a short letter: "As I have not given you a present this year, here are my wings. I hope you like them because I worked hard for them, and I am proud of them."

At the Princess' London house, in Belgravia, the wings and the letter are pinned up on her dressing-room door, a token of Talal's unforgettable courage.

Gérard Boucheron
to Alain Boucheron

Top, Gérard Boucheron
Above, Alain Boucheron

Jewelry is the natural currency of affection between the Boucherons, scions of the renowned Parisian jewelers. Thus in 1980, when Alain Boucheron took over as president of the firm of Boucheron, which had been founded by his great-grandfather Frédéric Boucheron in 1858, he received from his father, Gérard Boucheron, the former president, an exquisite piece of jewelry, rich in associations. This piece, a brooch, was originally a token from Gérard's father, Louis Boucheron, to his wife on their twenty-fifth wedding anniversary, in 1925. Because she had blue eyes, the design features lapis lazuli, with accents of coral, jade, and small diamonds, all mounted

on yellow gold. Highly distinctive, it was a prototype for the style of jewelry that developed in the thirties.

This elegant period piece is a symbol of Boucheron's reputation for strong, pure design. It is particularly precious to Alain, since he dearly loved the grandmother who first wore it.

Louis Boucheron, who may have designed the heirloom brooch that has come down to his grandson Alain, has left to his family evidences of his other talents in a book of studies of animals, flowers, and landscapes. Alain received this book as a present from his father's sister.

Katy Kass
to Joan Collins

Superlatives cluster around the name and person of Joan Collins, internationally famous film star and superstar of television. But lights, camera, and action are just the backdrop for her clear, simple, homespun ideas on children and gifts:

"As a mother, I am no exception to the rule; I think that one's children are the most precious possessions in life. Since their infancy, I have encouraged my children to believe that a gift that they make with their hands and their hearts is far more precious to me than something bought in a shop.

"I have received wonderful gifts from my three children, Tara, Sacha, and Katy, throughout the years. Paintings, drawings, handmade vases, poems, special photographs taken and developed by themselves, tapes of songs they have written and sung—all manner of lovely and original things.

"A little drawing and poem given me by my younger daughter, Katy, for my birthday in 1986 is very special to me. She adores Pierrot and Pierrette characters, as I do, and we both collect them. I loved her card and the sentiment expressed so much that I framed it and gave it pride of place on my study wall. Whenever I look at it, it reminds me of my darling Katy and the love we have for each other."

Above, Joan Collins and her daughter Katy Kass

Carlo and Sasha Gebler
to Edna O'Brien

Edna O'Brien, the Irish best-selling fiction writer and playwright reports: "The most bewitching present that I ever received was from my sons, Carlo and Sasha, when they were aged eight and ten respectively. It is the Book of Common Prayer and it has a silver cover depicting a coach and horses departing from church, with cyprus trees thrusting toward the sky. The principal thing about this book is its size—it is only three inches by two—truly for a Lilliputian. Consequently, the print is minute. I couldn't read it then, and I certainly can't read it now. The

flyleaf is inscribed, 'Sybil, with best wishes from Helen 4/2/05.' Where the boys found it I will never know, but since they were not very flush I imagine it was a bargain at some fête or other. I treasure it as a little talisman and because of its size it always accompanies me on my travels."

Carlo and Sasha Gebler are the sons of Edna O'Brien's early marriage to the writer Ernest Gebler. Carlo is an accomplished novelist, and Sasha a successful architect. Both live and work in Britain.

Charles de Gaulle
to His Grandson Charles de Gaulle

The Charles de Gaulle who was born in 1947 bears an illustrious name—the name of a leader whose statesmanship, he feels, can be compared to that of Louis XIV and Napoleon.

The eldest of four sons, this Charles de Gaulle, named for his grandfather, had a special place in his affections. From ten years of weekly family lunches at the Palais de l'Elysée during de Gaulle's presidency (1959–69) and vacations spent at the family house at Colombey-les-deux Eglises, many memories but only two actual mementos have been garnered. Both are objects that the young de Gaulle admired. In both instances the grandfatherly response was, "Would you like to have it?"

One of the gifts is a model of a junk (the sailboat of Oriental waters) with a cargo of pots, jars, and jugs. The other is a curved, gold-plated sword with a jewel-encrusted handle and an inscription in Arabic. These exotic remembrances, calculated to stir the imagination of a young boy, are specially treasured because of the loss of many other heirlooms during the Occupation.

The Honourable Jacob Rothschild
to His Daughter Hannah

Hannah Rothschild's safe return from a journey to India was the occasion for a gift from her father that is one of her greatest personal treasures and a favorite conversation piece. Its strange history is a reminder of the legendary era when the rulers of India's princely states could command the fulfillment of any whim, no matter how bizarre.

It was in those halcyon days that an eccentric Maharajah of Gwalior (he is said to have had his after-dinner cigars delivered to him by a model railroad that he had set up in his palace) became so passionately attached to his Lincoln Continental, named "The Pride of Gwalior," that he ordered a phonograph made in its image.

The Maharajah's fortunes dwindled, but the phonograph-automobile miraculously survived. It was next heard of some thirty years later, when an antique dealer in London received from India a mysterious telegram saying SEND ONE HUNDRED POUNDS (£100) AND AWAIT SURPRISE. The London dealer was indeed surprised. He was also fortunate, for the curious artifact subsequently caught the eye—and the fancy—of Jacob Rothschild, the eminent British financier.

Hannah Rothschild's odd and entertaining gift—which surely adds a new dimension to the term "audio-visual"—is installed in her parents' house, Stowell Park, in Wiltshire.

Corrado Pesci
to Virna Lisi

In 1968, when he was six years old, Virna Lisi's son, Corrado Pesci, asked her what was the most important prize that could be won by the best actress in the world. Heroine of countless Italian films and many international films, and winner of many accolades, Virna Lisi told little Corrado about the Oscar.

At Corrado's school in Italy it was a Christmas custom for the children to make a drawing for their father and mother, put it into a sealed envelope, and place it under their parents' plates at Christmas dinner, to be opened with due ceremony.

That year, young Corrado decided to do his utmost to give his mother an Oscar. His Christmas drawing showed her holding in her hand the little gold man of her description, with numerous figures applauding, and the words "Brava, brava Virna" and "Brava Mama" written boldly all over.

Virna Lisi has never forgotten her feeling of pride and wonderment at her little boy's going to such lengths to please her, at an age when most children's imaginings are limited to little houses or Christmas trees. Some eighteen years later, in 1986, she commented, "I have had many presents from my husband, from everybody, but this little drawing is for me the most important."

Cassian, Damian, and Cary Elwes
to Tessa Kennedy

Tessa Kennedy has an unusual collection of gifts from her three eldest sons. Each symbolizes a first or early step toward the achievement of a goal in a chosen field of creativity. All three young men—Cassian, a film producer, Damian, an artist, and Cary, an actor—give evidence of their artistic inheritance. Their late father, Dominic Elwes, was an artist. Their grandfather, Simon Elwes, was renowned as a portrait painter. Tessa Kennedy has made a name for herself as a peripatetic interior designer; her numerous glamorous assignments have included Stavros Niarchos's yacht and a house in the south of France for film producer Sam Spiegel.

Cassian, aged twenty-seven, gave his mother a poster of his first picture (as co-producer), *Oxford Blues*, made for MGM, in which his younger brother Cary played a part. Damian, aged twenty-six, presented her with a set of "artist's mother's" proofs of the lithographs shown at his inaugural exhibition, held at the Tricycle Theatre gallery. From Cary, aged twenty-three, have come a copy of the first published review of a stage performance of his as a pupil at Harrow, a notice of his part in Agatha Christie's play *A Spider's Web*, and props from his first West End stage success—*Another Country*, by Julian Mitchell—a cricket ball and a white silk scarf.

All these remembrances are regarded by Tessa Kennedy with deep sentiment for the love that they express and for their affirmation of her early belief in the boys' abilities. "To see them blossom so very, very fast is an incredible delight."

*Tessa Kennedy's sons Damian, Cary, and
Cassian Elwes with younger siblings*

Jean-Yves and Hubert Lanvin
to Bernard Lanvin

One of the most durable traditions in French haute couture was established by Jeanne Lanvin (1867–1946), and the Lanvin saga is as vigorous as ever under the direction of Bernard Lanvin. A constant search for memorabilia of Jeanne Lanvin is one of Bernard Lanvin's many activities. The famous portrait of her by Edouard Vuillard, of which the family possesses the artist's *esquisse* (sketch), is in the collection of the new Musée d'Orsay in Paris.

An important addition to the Lanvin museum came about through the perspicacity of the youngest generation of Lanvins, Bernard's sons, Jean-Yves and Hubert. They have always been encouraged by their parents "to know the world in which we are living" through travel, the theater, the opera, the ballet, and even through the auction markets.

At their very first auction Jean-Yves and Hubert saw a painting of Jeanne Lanvin coming through, and, inexperienced though they were, they took a chance and bid for it. Fortunately, their bid was successful.

And the timing was perfect: they were able to present to their father for Father's Day a much-appreciated gift —a portrait by Jean Dunan, probably painted in 1917, showing Jeanne Lanvin at about the age of fifty.

Above, Jeanne Lanvin with a model

Evelyn Waugh
to Auberon Waugh

Auberon Waugh, novelist, critic, commentator, and editor of Britain's periodical *The Literary Review,* gives a terse account of a gift from his distinguished father, Evelyn Waugh (1903–1966): "The story of this object is that it is an antique silver-and-onyx snuffbox belonging to Dr. Alexander Waugh, who was a medical practitioner in North Somerset in the village of Midsomer Norton. It was my great-grandfather's snuffbox. My father got it from his father, who got it from his father, who got it from his father. It was a sort of family heirloom. My father gave it to me when I was about twelve years old in order to encourage me to take snuff and to discourage me from smoking cigarettes. The box is my proudest possession, but it never walked at all: I have not stopped smoking cigarettes from that day on."

John, 2nd Lord Montagu of Beaulieu, to His Son, Edward, the 3rd Baron

the legendary Rolls-Royce hood ornament. The car had already been in production for four years when the manager of the company, Paul Johnson, appealed to his good friend for help in finding "a really dignified mascot." Lord Montagu suggested that Charles Sykes, art editor of *The Car Illustrated*, be commissioned to design an

The picturesque old Hampshire village of Beaulieu, where the Montagu family have lived since 1538, has among its modern attractions the National Motor Museum, founded by the present Lord Montagu of Beaulieu. Both the village and Lord Montagu come by their interest in the automobile honestly. John Douglas-Scott Montagu, the 2nd Baron Montagu of Beaulieu (1866–1929), was one of the very early motorists in Great Britain: he was a champion of the new invention when motorcars were being attacked as "juggernauts of the devil"; in 1899 he took the Prince of Wales (soon to be Edward VII) for his first ride; as a member of Parliament in 1904 he introduced the bill for the adoption of license plates; and he founded the weekly *The Car Illustrated* (1902).

Lord Montagu also played a part in the creation of

appropriate symbol. The little silver sprite that artist Sykes conceived, called "The Spirit of Ecstasy," was modeled by Eleanor Thornton, who was Lord Montagu's assistant and his great love. At the same time Sykes designed for Lord Montagu's own car a version of the little figure with her finger to her lips to indicate the quietness of the engine. "The Whisperer," as this sprite was called, was left by Lord Montagu to his son. It is a memento fraught with tender and tragic memories. When World War I broke out, Lord Montagu was required, as a military adviser, to go back and forth to India, and on December 30, 1915, the ship carrying him and Eleanor Thornton was torpedoed. Lord Montagu survived miraculously after drifting for three days in an open boat, but Eleanor Thornton, the inspiration for generations of silver sprites, was lost.

Viscount Linley
to the Earl of Snowdon

A distinct advantage of being a craftsman is that one can produce fine gifts for family and friends. David Linley, a young furniture designer, for his father's birthday in 1981 presented him with a beautiful little trinket box, made of the finest materials, that he had crafted himself.

David Linley chose this piece because it was the first of his efforts as a student at the John Makepeace School for Craftsmen in Wood, at Parnham House, Dorset, that had come close to the standards he aimed at. Also, "I knew that Papa would appreciate it," he says.

The box, wrought in sycamore, rosewood, ebony, and ivory, has three compartments. The designer recalls, "It took me about six weeks to complete. There was a considerable amount of dovetailing, and I did a lot of fidgety work with a sixteenth-of-an-inch chisel." The bottom of the box bears the inscription "To darling Papa, lots of love, David. 1981."

In part, this memento delights the recipient because it signifies the continuity of a family predilection for good design. Snowdon, as well as being one of Britain's leading photographers, is himself also known as a designer, and his uncle Oliver Messel was an internationally known stage designer. David Linley is co-founder and chairman of David Linley Furniture Ltd, a London firm that carries out special commissions for a range of pieces, including desks, cabinets, tables, and folding chairs, in addition to creating distinguished desk-top appurtenances.

Snowdon's pleasure has as much to do with the quality of workmanship shown in the piece as with the sentiment it expresses. "The patience and time put into the craftsmanship fill me with pride and admiration. The materials have a nice tactile quality; the box feels good to open and shut. Like all good design, the box is simple and functional." He adds with great warmth, "I was thrilled that David gave it to me."

David's memento is proudly placed on his father's desk in his studio. Part of an arrangement of memorabilia, it sits not far from the limited-edition Wedgwood mug that Snowdon co-designed with Carl Toms (a British stage designer who worked with Oliver Messel) in commemoration of the investiture of the Prince of Wales at Caernarvon Castle in 1963. The mug is decorated with the badge of the Prince of Wales—the three feathers. The unusual style of the design is taken from an antique button found at Caernarvon Castle.

*David Linley (seated) and
partner Matthew Rice in showroom
of David Linley Furniture Ltd.*

Princess Gloria von Thurn und Taxis
to Prince Johannes
von Thurn und Taxis

To the world at large the sixtieth-birthday celebrations, extending over three days, that Princess Gloria von Thurn und Taxis held for her husband, Prince Johannes, at their five-hundred-room palace in Regensburg may have seemed just the latest and biggest high society extravaganza. In fact it represented Princess Gloria's well-thought-out credo of gift giving: "If I want to give a present to Johannes that is really a present, I'm not going to go and buy something, because that's too easy. . . . For me the only thing would be to give him something where direct work is really involved. So I thought that I would give

him a party—a party such as he had never seen before and that he won't see again. Luckily it succeeded." Not only Johannes but the 250 guests as well loved the fantasy that the party created of three days of living in the eighteenth century, climaxed by the opera *Don Giovanni* with a pop ending sung by Princess Gloria.

THE GIFT FOR AN OCCASION

Prince Johannes has his own credo about presents. "He is just somebody that likes to get away from rules," says Gloria. "He doesn't actually like giving gifts for occasions. . . . Two weeks after Christmas you get an incredible big present!" One of these is an exquisite necklace of sapphires, pearls, and diamonds that reflects the Prince's exceptional knowledge about jewelry, which he is gradually imparting to his wife. The Princess says that jewelry has become important to her chiefly because it is important to Johannes, yet on balance she ranks her sports car at the top of the gifts that he has given her!

Above, Prince and Princess von Thurn und Taxis

The task of fitting a present to an occasion has taxed human ingenuity at least since the days of the Three Wise Men. And there is no letup in this search: not only holidays, birthdays, betrothals, marriages, anniversaries, and other family events but also an increasing number of personal occasions in modern life call for the salute of a present. In the West we seem to relish the chance to mark every watershed and milestone in the life of an individual with a tangible gesture of generosity and the ceremony that goes with it. The ideal choice is clearly a gift that is appropriate for the occasion and embodies the particular predilections of the recipient. Surprisingly, people continue to succeed in finding "the very thing."

The empire of fashion shops in London, New York, Paris, and Tokyo headed by Joseph Ettedgui testify to his taste, his understanding of style, and his capacity for making decisions. Yet he has admitted that when it came to choosing a wedding present for his young bride, Sarah, he was beset by uncertainty.

One thing he was sure of was Sarah's interest in books and art. Since he himself had been collecting the American pop artist Jim Dine over the years, it occurred to him that a picture by Dine might be the answer. The fact that one of the artist's most frequently used motifs is the heart seemed an added recommendation in the circumstances. He whisked Sarah off to Dine's dealer in London and together they chose a Dine lithograph. "It seemed very appropriate," says Joseph. "The picture was of two strong hearts."

One man whose friends seem to have had the requisite sixth sense was composer, author, playwright, songwriter, actor, singer, director, producer, and entertainer Noël Coward. His private and his professional life were starred with celebratory events that were signalized in delightfully three-dimensional ways. Among his most cherished trophies were those presented to him on his seventieth birthday, in 1969, by members of the British royal family. The incomparably witty observer of the social scene wrote very simply about this occasion in his diaries: "My birthday lunch was given by the darling Queen Mother at Clarence House, where I received a jewel-encrusted cigarette box from her and an equally jewel-encrusted cigarette case from the Queen...." Coward also recalled the moment at lunch when the Queen asked him whether he would accept the Prime Minister's offer of a knighthood, and his answer: "I kissed her hand and said, in a rather strangulated voice, 'Yes, Ma'am!'"

More personal, and treasured for that very quality, were other gifts that Coward received at various times. Mary Martin, a needlepoint enthusiast, presented him

with a cushion immortalizing his one-act play *Hands Across the Sea*, first performed in London in 1936. The needlepoint design depicted two clasped hands, symbolizing both the theme of the play (friendship between America and Britain) and the personal relationship between actress and playwright. Dame Joan Sutherland, the Australian soprano, made him a needlepoint cushion that picked up on a childhood passion—never outgrown—for railway trains. Among Merle Oberon's offerings, in the 1960s, was a pair of green velvet slippers hand-embroidered with Coward's initials. From Frank Sinatra came a pair of gold-and-ebony monogrammed cuff links, from Marlene Dietrich a black-silk dressing gown and matching pajamas. David Niven gave him a Picasso ceramic plate, and Cecil Beaton presented him with a drawing portraying the playwright in a debonair mood, waving a cigarette.

The bounty provided by his friends meant a great deal to Coward, as is shown by his reaction to the loss of one such gift. Some time after Tallulah Bankhead asked for, and received back, the painting by Augustus John that she had given the playwright in gratitude for obtaining the part of Amanda in *Private Lives*, Elsa Maxwell, who was notorious for asking for the return of presents, gave him a gold cigarette case. Coward ensured the permanence of this gift by having it engraved with the words "For Noël from Elsa Maxwell."

Occasions bring out the special talent that theater people have for endowing art with permanence. In honor of his eightieth birthday, in 1985, Emlyn Williams was given an early photograph of the cast of his long-running drama *The Corn Is Green*, which opened at the Duchess Theatre in London in 1938. He had also directed the play and played a part in it. The shot had been taken by British theater photographer Angus McBean in the style of a Victorian daguerreotype, which conformed with the period in which the play was set. Williams recalls that when the picture was being taken, his fellow actors wanted him to be placed in the center of the group but he had insisted on the arrangement remaining faithful to the casting. He is thus shown in the corner in his role as a schoolboy. The photograph, which was presented to him by actor Victor Spinetti, a fellow Welshman, is signed by all the members of the cast: Sybil Thorndike, Kathleen Harrison, Frederick Lloyd, John Glyn Jones, Betty Jardine, Christine Silver, and Emlyn Williams, who comments, "It has tremendous sentimental value for me. It reminds me of people I knew and loved."

One of the happier aspects of Noël Coward's musical *The Girl Who Came to Supper*—which had a brilliant opening in New York at the huge Broadway Theatre in

Gifts to Noël Coward
from Queen Elizabeth the Queen Mother and Queen Elizabeth

Needlepoint cushions by Mary Martin and monogrammed slippers by Merle Oberon

Ceramic plate by Picasso and drawing of Noël Coward by Cecil Beaton

1963 but ran for only three months—was the opening-night gift presented to him by his friends actress Katharine Cornell and author and lyricist Nancy Hamilton.

The two women dressed up in Edwardian costumes from the show and sat for a special photograph, which was set in a curiously wrought frame made of silver dollars. The memento, dated 8 December 1963, was inscribed "Are the Girls to Stay?" and the words "Noël with love from Kit and Nan." Producer Herman Levin recalled Coward's delight in what he called "a wonderful picture."

Betrothals and weddings traditionally generate the most glamorous presents. When Prince Napoleon, Pretender to the Imperial Crown of France (to be distinguished from the Bourbon-Orléans royal claimant, the Comte de Paris), commissioned Jean Schlumberger to design a ring for his fiancée, the Prince, a descendant of Napoleon's youngest brother, Jérome, supplied the diamond, which had belonged to his great-great-aunt Josephine. For this historic special order the designer encircled the heirloom stone with small marquise diamonds in the form of tiny bees, the emblem of the empire. The Prince was extremely pleased with the effect and gave Schlumberger the right to duplicate the setting.

When Queen Elizabeth the Queen Mother, as Lady Elizabeth Bowes-Lyon, married the Duke of York (later George VI), in 1923, Queen Mary gave her new daughter-in-law a suite of sapphires and diamonds. She also made some generous gifts to Princess Elizabeth on her marriage to Prince Philip, in 1947. A vitrine filled with presents of jewelry was among the leading attractions of a public showing of the wedding presents (held in aid of a charity) at St. James's Palace, following the marriage of Princess Anne and Captain Mark Phillips, in 1973.

Among the rich and landed, the bestowal of a fine house on the occasion of marriage has always found favor. Of special Anglo-American importance was William Waldorf Astor's gift of Cliveden, his country seat in Buckinghamshire, to his eldest son, Waldorf Astor, when he married Virginia-born Nancy Langhorne in 1906. At Cliveden the Astors brought together leading figures in literature and politics, and it became a glittering powerhouse, wielding a great deal of influence. With Nancy Astor—who was elected to her husband's seat in the Commons when he succeeded his father as viscount and thus became the first woman to sit in Parliament—as their hostess, the so-called Cliveden Set was said by some to be running the country.

The wedding present given by Baron Enrico "Ricky" di Portanova to his bride, Alessandra, in 1973 was the fulfillment of her dream of building, in lower Las Brisas in Acapulco, "a slightly mad but essentially practical modern

Photograph of the cast of The Corn Is Green

Left, Photograph of Nancy Hamilton
and Katharine Cornell in silver-dollar frame

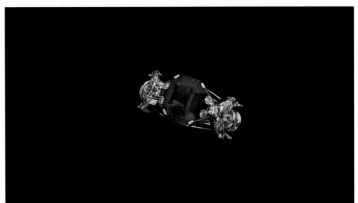

Above top, Ring designed for the fiancée of
Prince Napoleon by Jean Schlumberger

Above, Cliveden in Buckinghamshire,
country seat of the Astors

Crystal marriage goblets presented to
the Duke and Duchess of York
by President and Mrs. Reagan

The Crusaders, *crystal bowl presented by*
President and Mrs. Reagan to
the Prince and Princess of Wales

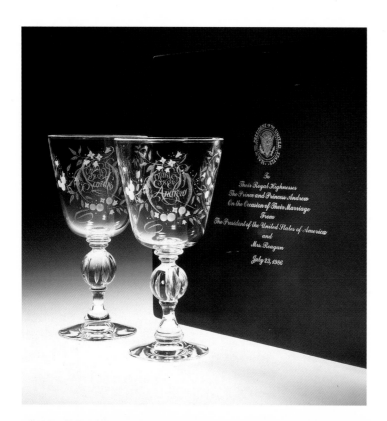

Crystal bowl and crystal candlesticks, wedding gift to
Princess Anne and Captain Mark Phillips
from President Nixon and the presidential family

house in the old tradition of the 'folly.' " The di Portanovas planned their project together, with the help of a draftsman. The architecture shows Mogul, Moorish, Islamic, and Venetian influences. The Villa Arabesque, with its 2½ acres, thirty-two rooms, thirty-eight bathrooms, three swimming pools, paddle-tennis court, nightclub, private beach, and heliport, has become famous for its originality and luxury.

At one stage during the development of the house Sandra realized that something was missing: although there were water effects such as little streams, pools, and cascades there was no waterfall. "I asked for a waterfall," she recalls, "but I forgot that when Ricky does things he does them in a big way. . . ." The entire façade of the house is a waterfall of some thirty feet!

The Baroness sees the whole domain as "a piece of living sculpture." The donor seems to have gained as much satisfaction out of the project as his wife, which is remarkable because, as he admits, "She talked me into it."

Marriage has rarely in modern times brought such magnificent quarters in its wake as in the case of the noted philanthropist and fund-raiser Florence van der Kemp, wife of Gérald van der Kemp, one of France's most distinguished museum directors, among whose titles is Conservateur en Chef du Musée National de Versailles. Mme. van der Kemp is quoted as saying that the only time her husband had given her anything was when he pinned the ribbon of the Légion d'Honneur on her at a big reception at Versailles—adding, "However, he gave me as a residence for twenty years the Château de Versailles."

A gift that recalls the arts of the past makes particular sense as a wedding present. The idea of tradition certainly entered into the choice of a present from President and Mrs. Reagan to the Duke and Duchess of York on their marriage, on July 23, 1986. This was a pair of blown crystal marriage goblets by Steuben decorated with diamond-point engraving, a revival of a sixteenth–seventeenth–century technique.

A historical theme also inspired the gift presented by President and Mrs. Reagan to H.R.H. the Prince of Wales and Lady Diana Spencer on the occasion of their marriage, on July 29, 1981. An elliptical crystal bowl, entitled *The Crusaders*, this Steuben piece was engraved by copper wheel to suggest a crusader's ship, with Richard the Lion-Hearted and his nobles preparing to disembark. The exceedingly rare type of copperwheel engraving used causes the figures to appear in high relief. The theme of the eagle, symbol both of royalty and of the United States, dominated the gift of Steuben glass presented to H.R.H. Princess Anne on the occasion of her marriage to Captain

Baron and Baroness di Portanova at Villa Arabesque

Adnan Khashoggi and Bob Shaheen

Silver cowbell with inscription by Richard Harris

Mark Phillips, on November 14, 1973, by President Nixon and the presidential family: a flared crystal bowl, supported by four gold eagles standing on a gold base inlaid with malachite, and four crystal candlesticks.

If statistics are any guide, there may well be a promising future for divorce presents. In the nature of things, they may entail less fanfare but more imagination. Richard Harris, of *Camelot* fame, presented his wife, Elizabeth, with an old Irish silver cowbell during their divorce, in 1968. It was inscribed "Now wherever you go, I will know where you are," and has traveled with her to homes in Italy, France, and America. "It must have been a very special cow that wore that bell," remarks Elizabeth. "We always had a very good relationship, and still have. Richard is my greatest friend." At the same time Elizabeth gave Richard a small caged bird in silver inscribed "Here is one bird that won't get away."

There already exists a friendly trend toward post-divorce mementos. Brigitte Bardot includes among her spoils a present from ex-husband Gunther Sachs given some years after their two-year marriage had ended. Rolf Sachs, Gunther's son, explains that the present was prompted by the fact that his playboy-industrialist father had just pulled off an international financial deal: "He became very, very well known through his marriage to Brigitte Bardot, and this helped to push through the negotiations." The present was "a big, beautiful diamond," quite as fine as anything Sachs might have given Brigitte during their married days.

Birthdays call for imagination on the part of the giver, since the day keeps coming around. Spoken and printed birthday wishes are all very well, but these lack the resonance of the greeting that awaited Baroness Tita Thyssen-Bornemisza on April 23, 1984. The Baroness, wife of industrialist and art collector Baron Hans Heinrich Thyssen-Bornemisza, was at home, sitting on the verandah of the Villa Favorita on Lake Lugano, when the telephone rang. She answered to hear the world-famous voice of Plácido Domingo in an operatic rendering of "Happy Birthday." The following year the renowned Spanish tenor José Carreras called and serenaded the Baroness on her natal day.

Birthdays and hats seem to go together. Maurice Chevalier apparently thought so when at a party in Paris for Duke Ellington's seventieth birthday he presented his famous theater prop—his straw boater—to the Jazz King. Lady Diana Cooper, almost as far-famed for the gifts that were showered upon her as for her beauty and intelligence, was given a charming embroidered shade hat set about with iced cakes at a birthday celebration when she was in her eighties. It was a present from Nigel Ryan, a senior executive with Thames Television in Britain.

In a long-standing friendship, the exchange of birthday presents can achieve the status of a game—a game whose playing gives as much, or almost as much, satisfaction as the tangible rewards involved. A classic instance is Adnan M. Khashoggi's engagement in a tussle of wits with his devoted chief of staff, Robert Shaheen. Years ago, the Saudi Arabian entrepreneur started the custom of giving Shaheen a birthday present amounting to one thousand times his age, paid in the standard unit of currency of whichever country the much-traveled pair happened to be in on the day of the anniversary. The aide's strategy had been to try to maneuver his schedule so that he would spend his birthday within the boundaries of a country, such as the United States or Britain, whose currency had a high value; Khashoggi's ploy was to effect the opposite.

One year, A.K., as he is called by his staff, had his lieutenant trapped in his yacht in Istanbul harbor. As the day approached, it looked as if the birthday boy was going to be lumped with thousands of feeble Turkish lire. However, on the day, Shaheen managed to lure the ship's captain into a celebratory sail beyond the three-mile limit. One up for Shaheen: in international waters the dollar is king. Another year, Shaheen was convinced that he had his employer by the high-currency tail: the two men were relaxing at Khashoggi's estate in the Canary Islands when Shaheen brought up the fact that on the following day, which happened to be his birthday, they were due to meet a group of lawyers in London. Khashoggi adroitly directed that his private plane be sent to the capital to bring the lawyers back to the island for the meeting. In a move that was to prove fruitless, Shaheen reminded his chief of the unjustifiably high cost of this proposed change of plan. "On birthdays," responded Khashoggi, "you sometimes have to spend money in order to save money."

Here and there a present has been known to make its way to its destined owner through a labyrinthine series of events. Kingman Brewster, Master of University College, Oxford University, can bear witness to this. In 1971 on a visit to Christ Church College at Oxford, Brewster, then President of Yale University, saw a sterling silver rampant yale at the High Table in the dining hall. Since the yale, a mythical beast that is a combination of bull, lion, and horse, is the friendly mascot of Yale University, the Master of Christ Church, Lord Todd, it was reported, said that he had had the sculpture nailed down when he heard that Brewster was coming to the college. However, Brewster was satisfied merely to admire the piece. About six years later, at the American Embassy in London—he had been appointed Ambassador to Great Britain by President

The Kingman Brewsters' silver rampant yale

Carter in 1977—Brewster received a call from a friend of the sculptor of the Christ Church yale (it had been given to the college in honor of the caller's father). He had heard of the Ambassador's admiration for the piece, and he relayed the message that the sculptor would be happy to do one like it specially for the Ambassador. Most opportunely, his wife's birthday was coming up, and Kingman Brewster was able to present the new silver yale to Mary Louise. The Brewsters "have a wonderful time with it. It is about a foot high and stands on a beautiful stone base. It is full of spirit."

Gifts that add to the sheer enjoyment of living are rarer than they should be. In this category are presents of domestic animals, which increase the common stock of affection between human beings and the natural world. A black retriever named Bonnie has transformed at least one aspect of the life of British actress Diana Rigg. A gift from her husband, theatrical producer Archibald Stirling, the dog, sporting a big red bow on her head, awaited her new owner sitting on the grass outside the Stirlings' country seat in Scotland, at Christmas in 1984. Thanks to Bonnie, a gundog bred at Kelvinhead kennels and trained by Ron Montgomery in Scotland, Diana Rigg has a new attitude toward shooting parties. Not a shot herself, she frequently accompanies her husband and their friends on shoots, and has this to say: "A woman going out on a shoot is likely to find it cold, wet, and dull. You are expected to be a 'butt bunny.' [The butt is a stand, screened by low turf or a stone wall, where people gather during shoots to talk or to eat.] Now I work with my dog and I have a wonderful day. She is a brilliant retriever, and as she retrieves only with me, I am the object of her affections."

Gifts of food and hospitality are part of the culture of present giving. Undoubtedly, chefs have a strong lead in this department. Anton Mosimann, maître chef de cuisine at the Dorchester Hotel, Park Lane, and author of successful cookbooks, tells of welcoming distinguished guest Herbert von Karajan to the Dorchester by serving him—with the compliments of the chef—the maestro's favorite delicacy, tête de veau. (Mosimann had first learned of von Karajan's liking for the dish while working under a chef at the Palace Hotel in Lucerne, where the conductor stayed regularly.) Along with grateful thanks, Mosimann received from the maestro an astonished inquiry as to how on earth his taste for tête de veau had been discovered.

A paper knife does not seem, on the face of it, to represent a particularly imaginative choice. However in certain circumstances it can be regarded as a boon by the recipient. That is how James Galway, internationally acclaimed flautist and recording artist, feels about the paper knife with silver blade given him by his wife, Jeanne, for his birthday in December 1984, the first present that she had given him since their marriage a few months earlier. The British musician uses the paper knife to open his extensive fan mail, which he likes to deal with personally when he is at his house in Lucerne. "It is very important for a flautist's fingers to be protected," notes Jeanne. "Using the paper knife saves James from paper cuts."

In searching for a present for Prince Johannes Thurn und Taxis, as a thank-you for a cruise on his boat, *L'Aiglon*, in 1984, Prince Pierre d'Arenberg found a solution to the problem of choosing a gift for the person who really "has everything." He took a good photograph of the boat in full sail to Hermès in Paris, and they reproduced the picture, with the name of the boat above it, on the bowl of one of their famous ashtrays. Prince Pierre d'Arenberg had such success with this idea that he later commissioned for his sailing friend an ashtray portraying the Thurn und Taxis residence, the palace in Regensburg. The birthday of Princess Teresa von Furstenberg, first wife of Baron Thyssen-Bornemisza, gave Prince Pierre a perfect opening for the Hermès ashtray gift. The Princess had sent out an invitation decorated with a trompe l'oeil view of her fantastic castle on the Danube. She was "absolutely overjoyed" with the reproduction of this view on the ashtray. The Prince's grandmother, Mrs. Frederick Bedford, was delighted with his choice of a design for her. This depicted her antique creamy-white Mercedes-Benz SSK, circa 1924, which according to the Prince was the one possession that she really cared about.

When Lord Howard de Walden's racehorse Slip Anchor won the Derby, in 1985, Lady Howard de Walden devised a lavish and highly appropriate gift in honor of the splendid victory. She commissioned Cartier to design for her husband a pair of platinum cuff links with a diamond cut in the shape of a horse's head on one side of each link and on the other, outlined in baguette diamonds, an anchor, echoing the nautical name of the winning steed.

The notion of commissioning a truly hideous object as a Christmas present is just one more quirky footnote in the history of the elegant Fifth Avenue firm of Cartier. The idiosyncratic Prince Constantin Radziwill, obliged to give a memento to a disliked relation, once placed an order for "the ugliest object in the world." The request was made to Cartier's clock department, which had long been at the service of eccentric customers. To the Prince's entire satisfaction, Cartier made him a clock in the form of a Swiss chalet in gold and diamonds with a cuckoo to strike the hours.

Lord Howard de Walden's cuff links

Diana Rigg's black Labrador retriever

Vivien Leigh
to Sir Anthony Quayle

The world fame of Vivien Leigh rests securely on her delicate beauty and her acting skill. Sir Anthony Quayle adds a sidelight. "Vivien," he says, "was famous for the thought and care she put into opening-night presents." Sir Anthony has proof of this in a keepsake Vivien gave him in 1955, when they, along with Laurence Olivier (then Vivien's husband), were playing in *Titus Andronicus* at Stratford on Avon. Sir Anthony played the part of Aaron the Moor in this Royal Shakespeare Company production.

The memento is a small intaglio carnelian seal depicting a black slave kneeling with his hands shackled, and bearing the inscription "Am I not a man and a brother?" This seal became the emblem of the Slave Emancipation Society, and was widely reproduced during the campaign for the abolition of the slave trade and of slavery itself led by the British politician and humanitarian William Wilberforce (1759–1833). Many hundreds of medallions of the seal were made by Wedgwood and it became fashionable to wear them mounted on bracelets and hair ornaments.

Another opening-night present that means a lot to Anthony Quayle is the sword that the actor Charles Kemble (1775–1854) wore when he played the part of Coriolanus. The sword is engraved "Tony Quayle from John Gielgud 1952."

Above, Vivien Leigh
photographed by Jean Howard

Opposite
Anthony Quayle as Aaron, the Moor

Baron and Baronne Guy de Rothschild to President Georges Pompidou

In his book of memoirs, *The Whims of Fortune*, Guy de Rothschild gives this amusing account of a comedy of errors involving a Christmas present:

It happened in 1973. Christmas was drawing near. Marie-Hélène had not yet found a present for Georges. A true perfectionist, she enjoys nothing more than unearthing the object that will give the greatest pleasure. She returned home triumphantly one evening and showed me a work by the sculptor François-Xavier Lalanne. . . . It was a white porcelain duck, floating among metal waterlilies.

"And you know," Marie-Hélène said, "it's really a miracle! Only three copies exist. The Sèvres Museum bought one, and this was the last. It was already reserved, and I had to fight like a tiger to get it."

The next day, an enormous parcel was delivered and taken to the pink room to await the Christmas-wrapping ritual—a procedure that is one of Marie-Hélène's favorite follies: Two or three of the staff, surrounded by masses of wrapping paper and ribbons, are kept busy preparing the beautiful packages that will be piled underneath the Christmas tree at Ferrières.

On December 23, an Ionesco-style dialogue took place among Marie-Hélène, the children's nanny, and the chauffeur:

"Juliette, will you please have Monsieur Pompidou's duck brought here?"

"But madame, the duck is already at Ferrières. I saw it there yesterday."

"That's impossible, Juliette, it's in the pink room. Pierre, did you deliver a brown parcel some six feet long and four feet wide to Ferrières?"

"No, madame . . ."

"You see, Juliette, the duck can't have walked there or flown to the chateau on its own wings!"

"I assure you, madame, it's there. I saw it."

Anger, threats of resignation. Both were adamant.

That same evening, Marie-Hélène went to Ferrières and had to accept the evidence: The duck was there. . ., patiently waiting to be gift-wrapped.

But the next morning, the duck had the last laugh: It was still waiting, just as patiently, but this time in a corner of the pink room in Paris! And the solution to the mystery was clear: Georges Pompidou had chosen the same duck, the third one, for us, and had had it delivered to Ferrières. . . .

Karl Lagerfeld
to Carla Fendi

A vintage watch by Piaget that Carla Fendi (one of the five sisters who head the noted fashion house of Fendi in Rome) has had for a few years but wears only on special occasions was a gift from a very special person, Karl Lagerfeld. Self-described as a "one-man international fashion phenomenon," Lagerfeld has had his own label since 1984 and has been connected with some of the biggest names in couture, not excluding Fendi. Carla, a great admirer of Lagerfeld's "classical and impeccable style," noticed this wonderful Piaget watch on his wrist and admired it. "I had to stop him from taking it off his wrist and giving it to me on the spot," Carla recalls. "Then it became a sort of game between us: his wanting me to accept it and my refusing to do so, until one day I told him that I could accept it only on that memorable day when Karl would have designed his first ready-to-wear collection for Fendi. In those years he was bound to other contracts, and so time passed and I completely forgot about that romantic pledge."

The day came when Karl did walk down the runway of the annual Milano Collezioni having designed his first ready-to-wear collection for Fendi. Carla describes the sequel: "The joy and relief of those moments, thanking the audience after a successful defile, are indescribable. While I was going backstage with Karl, still dizzy with emotion, I felt something being put hastily into my hand. It was the watch—the promised watch!"

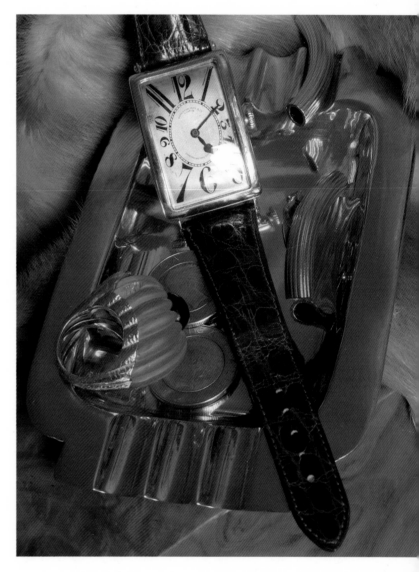

Carla Fendi and Karl Lagerfeld

Pope John Paul II
to Luciano Pavarotti

The silver-throated Italian tenor Luciano Pavarotti describes with feeling the circumstances surrounding a most memorable gift, presented to him in the hallowed precincts of the Vatican:

"One of the greatest emotional experiences of my life was an audience with His Holiness Pope John Paul II in June 1986. We met, together with the directors of the Teatro di Genova and the young singers who had been the winners of the second Luciano Pavarotti/Opera Company of Philadelphia International Voice Competition. [These singers had performed in a production of *La Bohème* at the theater in Genoa.]

"The occasion for this encounter was a journey: we were all leaving for China, a big, far-away country that we were to visit as ambassadors of the Italian people, committed to brotherhood with the Chinese people through the international language of music. Looking back at our trip, I think that we were successful in our mission.

"Before we left, we all met with the Pope, and he blessed our expedition. Our meeting did not last long, but the atmosphere became magic. When I think back to it, I get goose pimples!

"As if the meeting and his blessing and best wishes were not enough, the Pope gave me a rosary of exquisite simplicity that I treasure jealously. I take it with me always as a symbol of peace, love, and faith."

Above, Luciano Pavarotti and
Pope John Paul II

Carol Price
to Ambassador Charles H. Price II

From his vantage point as a ranking diplomat, Charles H. Price II, United States Ambassador to the Court of St. James's, credits his wife, Carol, with a distinctive flair in her choice of gifts, whether for him and their children or for their many friends and associates.

To mark the occasion when the Ambassador presented his credentials to the Court of St. James's, on December 20, 1983, Carol Price devised a collection of celebratory presents. As a theme she chose the ambassadorial seal. Among the variations were a graceful Waterford cut-glass chalice with the seal splendidly

engraved and the Ambassador's name, the occasion, and the date inscribed by David Powell; a silver box decorated with a gold medallion of the seal (the inside was inscribed in Mrs. Price's handwriting "To Charlie, my ambassador par excellence"); a silver-framed news photo of the Ambassador outside the American Embassy on the way to Buckingham Palace for the presentation; and a needle-point cushion worked in a design based on emblems from the seal.

Clearly Mrs. Price adds to the taste of a connoisseur a fund of enthusiasm and firm adherence to her guiding principle, "Sentiment and meaning count most."

Above, Ambassador and Mrs. Charles H. Price II

Dr. Miriam Stoppard
to Tom Stoppard

A stage production is in large part ephemeral: after the final curtain comes down, the only record that remains for posterity is the script. Dr. Miriam Stoppard, wife of British playwright Tom Stoppard, had the imaginative idea of celebrating the opening of two of her husband's plays by presenting him with gifts that would perpetuate the plays' situations, lines, and stage business.

Francis Hewlett, a leading British artist and craftsman, executed a series of small ceramic sculptures representing lines or moments in each play. On the opening night of *Night and Day* (Phoenix Theatre, November 1978) Tom Stoppard received ten of these small sculptures; on the opening night of *The Real Thing* (Strand Theatre, November 1982) there were twelve. The artist had marked every piece with the page number of the speech that inspired it. "All these objects are like moments in the play," the playwright says. "They really are unique." Some literal, some surreal, they succeed in capturing the wit and subtlety of Tom Stoppard's writing.

Sir Roger Bannister
to Sebastian Coe

When, in 1954, Sir Roger Bannister became the first person to run the mile in under 4 minutes, Sebastian Coe, future two-time British Olympic gold medalist in the metric mile (1,500 meters) had not yet been born. By a striking coincidence, in 1979, just twenty-five years after Sir Roger's sensational achievement, twenty-three-year-old Sebastian Coe broke the existing one-mile record and brought the mile world's record back to Britain. This feat did not go unnoticed by Sir Roger. Coe soon received from him a letter of congratulation and a blue necktie.

It seems that in 1954 Sir Roger had commissioned a number of blue ties to commemorate his famous run and had presented most of them to people associated with that event, reserving a few to serve as awards. Coe received the last remaining tie. He explains what it meant to him: "Bannister in miling terms broke the big barrier—the physical barrier and the mental barrier of the first 4 minutes. A 4-minute mile is still a very high standard. To be given the tie—to be recognized by somebody of that standard in the sport—was a tremendous honor." The two athletes first met in that same year, 1979, when Sir Roger was presenting the trophy for the BBC Sports Personality of the Year to Coe—who recalls with chagrin that he forgot to wear the tie.

Comtesse Isabelle d'Ornano to Comte Hubert d'Ornano

Two handsome hand-decorated porcelain plates given by Comtesse Isabelle d'Ornano to her husband, Comte Hubert d'Ornano, French landowner, businessman, and noted sportsman, for Christmas in 1981 commemorate two sides of his life.

One is inscribed with "everything that has counted in our life together," says Isabelle d'Ornano, "our wedding day in Deauville, the names of our five children, the names of our different houses, the places we loved to go to, and the two cosmetic businesses which Hubert created, Orlane with his brother and Sisley with me." The other plate salutes Hubert d'Ornano as a sportsman. "He loves to shoot and has been to some of the best shoots in the world. And so written here for him are all the shoots he loves most," his wife points out. These include the three presidential shoots in France, Chambord for wild boar and deer and Marly and Rambouillet for pheasant; Helmsley, one of the best pheasant shoots in England; Grandlieu, the beautiful duck shoot of J.P. Guerlain in Brittany; Crag John Derby's grouse shoot in Yorkshire; Karvendel, the Rothschild mountain shoot in Austria; and Courance, the shoot of the Ganay family, near Paris.

Both plates are decorated with the d'Ornano coat of arms bearing the family device, *Deo favente comes Corsiae* ("By the grace of God, Count of Corsica"), and the motto *Point n'est besoin d'espérer pour entreprendre, ni de réussir pour persévérer*, which could be translated, "To venture unmindful of hope, to persevere unmindful of success." The designs were painted by an artist named Silvita Gallienne.

Cristóbal Balenciaga
to Hubert de Givenchy

Speaking of gifts, Hubert de Givenchy, master couturier (a retrospective exhibition of whose work was shown round the world in 1984), goes back to the year when he reached the age of thirty-two, the year 1957. A disciple of the great Balenciaga, Givenchy had by then headed his own house of couture for six years. His birthday, February 20, had already passed when his mentor remembered, expressed regret, and asked hesitantly if he had any idea of a gift that he would like. As Givenchy tells the story, the dialogue continued: "Cristóbal, what I want is for you to give me a dress."

"A dress!"

"Yes, because I admire your work—your style—so much."

When Balenciaga recovered from his astonishment he invited Givenchy to come to his showroom at 10, avenue George V to make a choice. Givenchy selected a yellow faille embroidered gown. "And it is the most extraordinary dress, you know, very very Balenciaga, absolutely beautiful!" Givenchy's unabated enthusiasm for the dress is, in retrospect, mingled with amusement at the idea of "one designer giving a dress to another."

Hubert de Givenchy

Fritz Kortner
to Klaus Maria Brandauer

Several of the great names in the venerable tradition of the Austrian theater figure in the story of a gift that Klaus Maria Brandauer received in 1973. Himself a noted actor in Austria, and more lately an international film star, Brandauer was in his early career a protégé of the renowned Austrian actor and director Fritz Kortner (1892–1970).

Kortner directed the young Brandauer in his acclaimed final stage production, Lessing's *Emilia Galotti*. Brandauer spent many hours in the company of the grand old man of the theater, and while visiting him he developed an attachment to a picture that hung over Kortner's desk. It was a lithograph portrait by the artist Ferdinand Schmutzer (1870–1928) of the famous actor Josef Kainz (1858–1910)—who was a favorite of Ludwig II of Bavaria and who has been called the greatest actor of his time—in the role of Romeo.

In 1973, three years after Kortner's death, Brandauer was playing his first Romeo at the Nationaltheater in Munich. On the opening night, the director's widow, Johanna Hofer, brought to his dressing room the much-admired portrait of Josef Kainz as Romeo. It was accompanied by a note from Kortner saying, "Take the picture, you deserve it." Klaus Brandauer recalls, "It was a wonderful moment, the best of omens for my performance."

The portrait of Kainz has a place of honor above Brandauer's desk in his apartment in Vienna.

Klaus Maria Brandauer

Diego Giacometti to César

César at work

French sculptor César and Italian artist-craftsman Diego Giacometti (brother of the sculptor Alberto Giacometti) were brought together fortuitously in the service of an

art—and an artist—far removed from their accustomed spheres. Both were enlisted in the designing of trophies to be awarded in memory of the noted French film producer Raoul Levy (1922–1966). The Raoul Levy Film Award, given yearly for outstanding merit in French film production, takes two forms: the bronze wolf designed by Giacometti alternates with the trophy designed by César.

Usually the annual award trophy is not signed by the artist. But Giacometti, inspired to make a private award, signed a bronze wolf and presented it to César, surprising and delighting his fellow trophy designer.

102

Kevin Coates
to Nel Coates

The first object that the versatile British musician and artist Kevin Coates made (albeit unknowingly at the time) for Nel Coates was a harpsichord. Indeed it was Nel's search for a harpsichord that led to their meeting, their marriage, and, eventually, their routine of starting the day with music—Nel at the harpsichord and Kevin playing either his baroque mandolin or his viola d'amore.

After this musical beginning, Nel tackles her work as an assistant producer for BBC's children's television and Kevin turns to his vocation as a gold- and silversmith and to the creation of imaginative objects that have won him a devoted following. For Nel he has made (in addition to

Kevin and Nel Coates

her wedding ring, which incorporates a hidden likeness of himself tucked beneath a star sapphire), a collection of jewelry and diminutive sculptures. Inspired by her elfin qualities, he has made her an elf of her own. A gold and moonstone ring that is one of Nel's favorite pieces represents the Egyptian falcon-god Horus. This and a brooch called "Days in Alexandria," which shows Nel framed in a window, refer to her childhood in Egypt. A gold faun, a silver "Cat Divinity," a harlequin-in-a-niche brooch are other pieces in Nel's collection. What delights her is that all these presents have been so much admired that they have spawned many similar works by the artist.

Ambassador Maxwell M. Rabb
to Ruth Rabb

One of the first unofficial acts of Maxwell Rabb after he was appointed United States Ambassador to Italy by President Reagan in 1982 was to present his wife, Ruth, with a gold pin in which the American ambassadorial seal is surrounded by thirteen red (ruby), white (diamond), and blue (sapphire) stones symbolizing the original thirteen states of the Union. The gift prompted the Ambassador's wife to say, "The pin has a special meaning for me. I really feel as if it is my badge of office."

Indeed the Rabbs' shared interest in public service is very much in evidence. Largely through Ruth Rabb's efforts a collaborative project between the Foundation for the Applied Arts of Fashion and Costume Design, in Florence, and the Fashion Institute of Technology, in New York, has been inaugurated. The school that was created, the International University of Fashion (Politecnico Internazionale della Moda), opened in Florence in October 1986, forming a bridge between the fashion worlds of Italy and the United States.

Earlier, Mrs. Rabb's interest in Italian artistry and craftsmanship had led her to discover in the beautiful cathedral town of Orvieto a little shop where a woodworker named Michelangeli made very appealing sculptural figures. She began to collect these dolls. Her collection was noted by, among others, the Rabbs' friend Marvin S. Traub of New York, Chairman and CEO of Bloomingdale's, and in the fall of 1985, when the Ambassador and his wife were guests of honor at the opening of the promotion called "Ecco l'Italia" at Bloomingdale's, Marvin Traub presented the Rabbs with dolls that had been specially made for them by Michelangeli.

Ruth Rabb's own gift to her husband on his appointment as Ambassador was an album of stamps calculated to delight his stamp collector's soul: a collection of stamps covering the entire history of the Republic of Italy from its beginnings to the present day.

Pierre Schlumberger
to São Schlumberger

São Schlumberger has a shining tale to tell about one particular memento bestowed upon her by her late husband, Pierre Schlumberger.

The occasion was her birthday in 1971, the fifteenth of October. "We were on a plane going to Spain for the shooting. My husband gave me a small brown paper bag and said, 'Here is your birthday present.' I was surprised and wondered what could be inside—nothing very special in such a wrapping, I imagined. What it contained was a small box. I opened it and almost fainted. Here was a 51-carat Golconda diamond from India. It had a remarkable

light. These diamonds are from mines in India that are now finished and they have a very special light in them; they don't look like a modern diamond from Africa. My birthday diamond has a name, 'El Mansour,' which in Arabic means 'The Victorious.'"

São Schlumberger adds by way of explanation, "My husband loved jewelry, and so he gave me what he liked." But indeed Pierre Schlumberger, in addition to being a sportsman and celebrated international host, was a connoisseur of art as well as of jewels, and the Schlumberger residence in Paris is graced with many artistic treasures.

Above, São Schlumberger

*Aniela and Arthur
Rubinstein*

Mme. Aniela Rubinstein
to Arthur Rubinstein

A great musician becomes, through his far-flung audiences, a citizen of the world. This was certainly true of the master pianist Arthur Rubinstein, who died in 1982 at the age of ninety-five. Rubinstein, born in Poland, had homes in Paris, Beverly Hills, and New York but he always bought his accustomed hat—a trilby—in London, at Lock's, the famous hatter on St. James's Street.

It is a favorite trilby (which he is said to have even worn indoors sometimes, as he couldn't bear drafts) that Mme. Rubinstein immortalized in a still life she painted as a present for him. She combined it with a favorite hat of her own, with colored ribbons, and a tuberose, the flower that her husband sent her on their wedding day. Mme. Rubinstein remembers that when she was painting the picture, in Marbella, Spain, her husband was "working on the Schubert sonata, the big one," and that is why the score is in the painting. Nela also occupied herself with handiwork during Arthur's long hours at the keyboard. On one fine linen handkerchief she embroidered the sentiment "With all my heart I wish you a happy eighties leading to a gay nineties."

Christopher Isherwood
and Don Bachardy
to Marguerite Littman

A long-standing friendship between the late Christopher Isherwood, Don Bachardy, and Marguerite Littman has inspired many remembrances, tangible and intangible.

The three met in California in the early fifties: the British/American novelist and poet (best known for his book *Goodbye to Berlin*, on which the musical *Cabaret* was based) and his friend Don Bachardy lived in Santa Monica, and Marguerite attended a summer session at UCLA. "The three of us have always taken our birthdays very seriously. We have called each other on our birthdays no matter where we were," says Marguerite, who lives in London with her husband, Mark, a director of the Rio Tinto-Zinc Corporation. Among her prized mementos in their house in Belgravia, a haven to many friends from abroad, is a miniature bureau that Isherwood and Bachardy gave her as a birthday present in the late fifties. "It is nineteenth-century—perhaps a tradesman's sample or made for a dollhouse. There were 'Happy Birthday' messages in each drawer. The bureau is symbolic, but the nicest thing is that they always remembered."

Jackie Stewart
to Helen Stewart

When Britain's ace racing driver Jackie Stewart retired in October 1973 (still holding the record for the most Grand Prix wins), to commemorate the event he presented his wife, Helen, with a choker necklace that celebrated his principal successes. Three strings of pearls recalled his three world championships. The clasp was made of a piece of metal from his helmet, enameled white and bearing the tartan design that was his insigne on the track. Ninety-nine small diamonds represent the number of Grand Prix races in which he had driven; twenty-seven small rubies stand for his twenty-seven victories. Comments Helen Stewart on her trophy: "I have worn it so often that I think Jackie is fed up seeing it on me!"

The notion that Helen Stewart had for marking the event commemorates her husband's achievements in a very different and very original way. She took one of his well-worn driving boots to Asprey's and had it dipped in silver—laces, scuffs, and all. The precious object was then set on a base with the inscription "To My World Champion, 1969, 1971, 1973."

Jackie Stewart notes with some pride, "It was the throttle-pedal boot—the one that did the damage. Under the silver there is a lot of sweat in that boot."

Helen and Jackie Stewart

As chairman of the elegant Bond Street jewelers, John Asprey is daily surrounded by precious objects. None has a more curious history than a beautiful Fabergé-style egg that stands on its gilded legs in his office.

It was to Asprey and Company that Albert R. "Cubby" Broccoli, producer of the James Bond film *Octopussy*, turned when he found that the script called for a Fabergé egg in several of the scenes; he commissioned the jewelers to create an egg in the style of the Russian master of the genre and to make three of them.

The film opened in London with a charity premiere and dinner dance, which Messrs. Broccoli and Asprey attended. One egg had been contributed by Cubby Broccoli to the raffle that was to be held after dinner. Hosting a table, John Asprey bought several raffle tickets for his guests. Roger Moore, who played James Bond, had the honor of drawing the tickets. He pulled out the first ticket and looked at the name: John Asprey. Thinking to avoid "carrying coals to Newcastle," he set the ticket aside and drew another.

The following day Broccoli came to John Asprey's office bearing the three eggs. Regretful that the true winner had not been awarded the prize, he offered him his choice and gave him the chosen egg as a present.

Czarina Alexandra Feodorovna
to Margaret Jackson

In 1900 Czarina Alexandra Feodorovna of Russia, then twenty-eight, gave to Margaret Jackson, the English-woman who had been her childhood governess, a gift that seems to have been a premonition.

The gift was a rock-crystal paper knife, or letter opener, from the House of Fabergé, court jewelers to the czars. In this Carl Fabergé piece, the smooth clarity of the natural stone, which so resembles glass, is set off by the goldsmith's work—a red-gold mount with a bowknot of ribbon and a pendant drop with one brilliant and four rose diamonds, set in silver, applied to a broad band of laurel chased in green gold. The handwritten note from the

Czarina, reading, "For dear Miss Jackson, with loving Xmas wishes from Alix, 1900," has been preserved along with the paper knife.

When, in 1917, during the Russian Revolution, the imperial family had been imprisoned, it was through Miss Jackson that the Czarina sent a letter to the British royal family. The missive was an urgent plea for help, containing plans of the house where the Romanovs were imprisoned. Whether Miss Jackson ever received a reply—and opened it with the Fabergé paper knife—will never be known, but history records that the Czarina and her family were executed by the Bolsheviks in 1918.

Giancarlo Giammetti
to Valentino

Choosing a gift for a person who has achieved as much in his field as Valentino, the great fashion designer, was a challenge that his longtime friend and business partner, Giancarlo Giammetti, met in an unusual and inventive way. It was his idea to commission Elena and Michel Gran, Russian artists working in Paris, to create a trompe l'oeil painting that would highlight Valentino's accomplishments and illustrate his life-style.

The picture, presented to Valentino in honor of the showing of his collection in Rome in January 1986, depicts an armoire to which are attached a variety of tangible references to significant things and events.

Here are the newspaper that Valentino reads every morning, *La Repubblica*; an old sketch by Valentino of

the Piazza Mignanelli, which he sees from his window; the initial V in a variety of styles; a bottle of the perfume named Valentino; a picture of Valentino's pug, Oliver; the book *Valentino*, published by Franco Maria Ricci; and a certificate from President Sandro Pertini making Valentino a Grande Ufficiale dell' Ordine al Merito de la Repubblica Italiana—one of the highest honors the nation can bestow.

The painting—with each object looking real enough to "fool the eye"—stands on an easel in Valentino's private office, Via Gregoriana 24. Tucked into a drawer of the trompe l'oeil armoire is a card whose inscription, "With a lot of wishes and much love, Giancarlo, 11 May 1986," is fully visible.

Above, Valentino and Giancarlo Giammetti

115

Lila de Nobili
to Leslie Caron

In 1962, the day after Leslie Caron received the British Academy Award for her performance in *The L-Shaped Room*, to mark the event her friend Lila de Nobili presented her with a painting of a little victory cherub that Leslie still speaks of in the most glowing terms: "I absolutely adore it."

The friendship between the actress and the painter of this cherished picture goes back many years. The two first met when Leslie Caron, about sixteen years old, was dancing in Roland Petit's Ballets des Champs Elysées in Paris. Lila de Nobili, herself very young, was designing sets and costumes.

When Leslie Caron married Peter Hall, then director of the Royal Shakespeare Company (later director of the National Theatre), she encouraged him to bring Lila ("He thought she was wonderful") to England to work with the company. Lila designed many productions for the R.S.C. and went on to become one of Europe's top stage designers, creating magnificent decors for the leading theaters, including the Paris Opéra and La Scala. Leslie Caron admires the character of her friend as well as her extraordinary talent. "Lila understood everything about life without having any herself. She dedicated all of herself to her sets, costumes, and designs—her work."

Above, Prince Philip and Leslie Caron

Ottavio Missoni
to the Marchese Franco Maria Ricci

The aristocratic Italian publisher of "the world's most beautiful magazine, *FMR*," wears on his lapel a plastic flower (a red gardenia, often called a rose) that has become his symbol, or trademark, even his signature.

The Marchese Franco Maria Ricci received the flower from the fashion designer Ottavio Missoni. He likes to tell the story of how in 1974, when Missoni was a new name, he offered those invited to his fashion show these red plastic flowers, which everybody disregarded. "I collected six or seven, and Missoni saw me and he put one on my jacket, saying, 'This is my gift.' And I went home with this rose, this gardenia, on my jacket, and the second day I was too lazy to take it out, and by the third day it was *my* flower. . . .

"So this little present from Missoni has become like no other object in my life. No other present has ever been so important for me, because it now coincides with me. It is like a uniform for a general. Now I keep it because I might become nothing without my rose!"

Hans Werner Henze
to Sir Yehudi Menuhin, O.M.

At a celebration in honor of his seventieth birthday, held in Bonn, West Germany, on June 1, 1986, Sir Yehudi Menuhin, one of the world's most celebrated violinists, received a gift of which he is especially proud. The event took Sir Yehudi completely by surprise; he knew in advance only that he and his wife were expected in the city that day.

Among the speakers were Helmut Schmidt, former Chancellor, who presented Sir Yehudi with the Grand Cross of the Order of Merit, Germany's highest honor, and Hans-Dietrich Genscher, Minister for Foreign Affairs. Then "one after another of my most beloved colleagues" played or spoke, to add to the delight of the recipient of this remarkable and completely unexpected tribute. From Hans Werner Henze, Germany's outstanding contemporary composer, came the ultimate gift that a composer can bestow upon a musician. Henze presented Sir Yehudi with a composition—Serenade for Solo Violin, to Celebrate 22 April 1916 (the actual birthday)—that he had written in his honor. The piece was performed by a talented young violinist, one of Sir Yehudi's pupils.

Franco Maria Ricci

Left, Sir Yehudi Menuhin, O.M.

Charles de Beistegui
to Hélène Rochas

Immortalized in countless memoirs, diaries, and photographs—and in the recollections of everyone who attended the affair—is the costume ball that Charles de Beistegui held on September 3, 1951, at his newly restored Palazzo Labia in Venice. A noted art collector, celebrated host, and pivotal figure in Europe's beau monde, de Beistegui planned this event as the ball of the century. High society from all parts of the world, including North and South America, came to Venice for the festivity. All the reigning beauties of the day were there, among them Hélène Rochas (who was the inspiration for the French company Parfums Rochas), Princess Natasha Paley, and Lady Diana Cooper, the hostess of the evening.

Hélène Rochas has a special reason for remembering the famous ball in the Palazzo Labia, for at Christmas that year, out of the blue, she received from the party's host the gift of a miniature silver slipper. The seeming allusion to the fairy tale of Cinderella was pleasant enough; what was even more pleasing was that her other friends began to follow suit. Over the years she has acquired a collection of diminutive silver slippers, some English, some Russian in origin, in a wide range of styles. Buckled and bowed, laced and tasseled, simple and elaborate, they are all redolent not only of Charles de Beistegui's ball but of her earliest love, the dance.

Above, Hélène Rochas

Prisoner
in a United States Penitentiary
to Gina Lollobrigida

What could a lone prisoner in a United States jail do during the long dark days to express his admiration for the glamorous Italian film star Gina Lollobrigida? As a metaphor for serenading her, he could—and did—make and send her a mandolin.

Of all the tributes that have been showered upon Lollobrigida by her fans, by the press, and by the pundits who make up the list of the Ten Most Beautiful Women in the World, this one holds a special place in her affections. "The mandolin arrived in a package at my place in Rome," she recalls, "with a letter from the sender, who

THE GIFT OF APPRECIATION

wrote that he admired me so much and that I was the prisoners' Queen." The mandolin is made entirely of used matchsticks—at least a thousand—all varnished and shaped into a full-sized instrument, with eight strings, that could really be played. This "very beautiful object" came to Lollobrigida, she adds, during the period when such of her films as *Trapeze, Solomon and Sheba,* and *Come September* were playing throughout the United States. Touched by the devotion of the prisoner and amazed by his skill in creating his gift without any tools, she dispatched a letter of gratitude to him, and the matchstick *mandolino* is kept among her personal belongings in her house in Rome.

Above, Gina Lollobrigida

Dr. Gianoli's watch with portrait of King Fahd

Miss Bluebell with Les Bluebell Girls

Some of the most appreciated presents are prompted by the giver's desire to show appreciation: muses and mentors, artists and patrons, magnates and maestros, kings and commoners alike are subject to the impulse to express gratitude in some tangible form. Often the sense of indebtedness acts as a liberator of the imagination. All manner of original gestures are made in the name of thanks.

Few offerings have exceeded in audacious charm the memento presented by Vivien Leigh to British photographer Angus McBean. The actress had set her heart on playing the role of Scarlett O'Hara in the film *Gone with the Wind*. The photographer had taken some shots of Vivien that she was eager to send to the agent Myron Selznick. She persuaded McBean to bring them to her cottage at Denham late one evening. They were shortly joined by Laurence Olivier, with whom the actress was then living. Angus McBean recalls that at the end of a day in which he had given two performances as Hamlet the actor was none too pleased to see him, and that Olivier was also irritated at Vivien's pursuing "a silly dream." As Angus left, the actress slipped a large envelope into his hand with instructions not to open it until later. Inside was a copy of *Gone with the Wind* inscribed "To darling Angus with love from Scarlett O'Hara, 1937." The photographs were forwarded, and eighteen months later Miss Leigh was conquering Atlanta.

There can be no more profound gratitude than that of an artist whose work is defended against the Philistines by a distinguished colleague. A touching example is Debussy's response to Arturo Toscanini's action at the Italian premiere in 1908 (at La Scala in Milan) of *Pelléas et Mélisande*, the only opera by the French composer. Debussy's sensuous, impressionistic score left the Italian audience cold, and during the performance heckling broke out. One particularly vociferous critic called out sarcastically, "Che bella musica!" Toscanini, without missing a beat, turned round and replied, "Si, si, per me, bella musica!" The fracas continued for about twenty minutes until the love scene, which earned a standing ovation. The audience was won over. At the end there were several curtain calls specifically for the conductor. Debussy, on hearing of this extraordinary incident, sent Toscanini a photograph of himself with the score of the love scene inscribed on it and, underneath, the words "This is where the tide turned."

In a comparable vein, Stephen Spender, British poet and literary critic, was determined that W. H. Auden's first volume of poetry, which had been rejected by several publishers, among them Faber & Faber (where T. S. Eliot was an editor), should see the light of print. As a labor of love, Spender undertook to set the book on his tiny Adana press, and he worked on it during the whole of the summer of 1928, until the press broke down. Even then, the book was not finished. Finally, after much effort and heartache, the Holywell Press in Oxford finished and bound the limited edition of some thirty copies, which it was the poet's pleasure to present to his family and to his friends. One can imagine the deep appreciation that accompanied the copy he gave his friend Stephen Spender.

A source par excellence of the gift of appreciation is the grateful patient. For Dr. Augusto Gianoli, the Swiss-based health guru with patients from all over the globe, grateful patients add up to a doctor's dilemma. Adnan Khashoggi, reputed to be one of the world's wealthiest men, who benefited from Dr. Gianoli's slimming regime, once told the doctor that he deserved to have a Rolls-Royce—and promptly bestowed one upon him. King Fahd of Saudi Arabia came to the doctor's clinic in Spain intending to stay for three weeks and remained for five weeks. In appreciation of a pleasant and successful stay and of the conversations that the two had enjoyed, he presented Dr. Gianoli with a white-gold Swiss watch, the case enhanced with some thirty diamonds, and a portrait of himself on the face.

A heartfelt token of appreciation was presented to Miss Bluebell, maîtresse de ballet of the celebrated troupe of dancers—Les Bluebell Girls—at Paris's popular nightclub the Lido. The fireman stationed in the building, Christian Perhusion, sought to borrow, for a charity show that he and his small group were organizing, some of the rhinestone-and-feather costumes worn by Les Bluebell Girls on stage. (The cost of hiring such magnificent attire was said to be in the region of 3,000–4,000 francs per dress.) When Miss Bluebell granted his request and told him that there would be no charge, the emotion of the moment silenced him. But later he bestowed upon his benefactor his proudest possession, his official fireman's insigne, specially mounted on solid oak.

Sentiments of appreciation felt by guests toward hosts have inspired many imaginative mementos, in addition to innumerable bouquets of flowers and thank-you notes. There have been times when the host has suggested the form of the memento. On one such occasion the late Andy Warhol was the guest of Paolo Marzotto, well-known dress manufacturer of Vicenza. The famous pop artist was served a typical Venetian lunch for the season; the menu included roast chestnuts and a wine, Reciolto della Valpolicella, produced in limited quantities by the host's friends Renzo and Lamberto Cesari at their estate, Brigaldara. Paolo Marzotto recalls

Giuliana di Camerino's bracelet with State of Texas charm

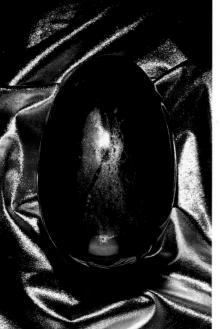

Naim Attallah's lapis lazuli egg

The Krokodiloes with Princess Manni Sayn-Wittgenstein-Sayn

that Andy Warhol enjoyed the chestnuts so much that he was moved to ask the artist to sign some, "in remembrance of the occasion when he first tasted this delicious fall fruit in Venice." Warhol obliged, which prompted Paolo to reflect subsequently that his distinguished guest should have been requested to sign the wine label as well.

Appreciation of enjoying the finest champagnes in Churchill's company tempered the long and often stormy relation between Lord Beaverbrook, Canadian politician and newspaper proprietor, and the British statesman. When Max Beaverbrook presented his drinking companion with one of the newly invented refrigerators, Sir Winston expressed his delight that he would no longer have to dilute his champagne with ice.

Chance led to a turning point in the work of Italian designer Giuliana di Camerino and to a token of appreciation from which she is rarely parted. Stanley Marcus, one of the great merchant princes of America, happened to notice an article on di Camerino in the magazine *Bellezza*. When he was next in Venice, he got in touch with the designer and it was he who took her to the fabric mills (suppliers to the Vatican) where Giuliana discovered the sumptuous cut velvets that inspired the handbag collection she launched in 1948/49—the Roberta di Camerino line. They were an immediate success on both sides of the Atlantic.

In 1956, Giuliana di Camerino received the prestigious Neiman-Marcus award, given for distinguished service in the field of fashion. The grateful designer says: "Stanley Marcus discovered me and he gave me a little gold charm in the shape of Texas. I always wear it because it brings me good luck. My first work, my first customer, my first real success came from Stanley Marcus and my beloved Texas."

Singing for one's supper is an old tradition; singing for one's honeymoon is a new idea—and one that only a person as imaginative and foresighted as Princess Manni Sayn-Wittgenstein-Sayn could have devised. The Austrian princess first heard the Harvard singing group known as the Krokodiloes when she was in New York. She invited the young men to be her guests at her residence in Fuschl, near Salzburg, if they would agree to give a concert. The group accepted with delight, stayed for three days, and gave a concert for fifty guests of the Princess. At the end of their visit, in a little speech expressing her appreciation to the singers, the Princess included a second invitation, reaching into the future. All these charming young men, she surmised, would marry. They would spend their honeymoons in expensive hotels like the Ritz in Paris and the Gritti in Venice, and they might very

well run out of money. They need never worry, said the Princess: each member of the Krokodiloes was welcome to spend a week in a snug cottage on her estate.

Although automobiles are not sentient beings, they have an almost human capacity to inspire sentiments of appreciation. An example is the vintage Morgan formerly owned by Richard Burt, United States Ambassador to West Germany. The Ambassador's wife, Gahl, recalls that when they first went out together it was frequently in the cherished Morgan, which Richard had bought in England when he was a *New York Times* foreign correspondent. On being posted to Bonn, the owner of the beloved Morgan, with great reluctance, made the decision to give it up. Not long afterward, Gahl Burt had the good fortune to discover in a flea market in Berlin a small picture frame made in the form of the front grille and headlights of the lamented Morgan. The little curio now frames a photograph of Richard's pride and joy and has a place of honor on his desk at the embassy.

In the competitive world of business there would seem to be little room for sentiment. Challenging this assumption is an enchanting memento treasured by Naim Attallah, the Financial Director of Asprey (who is also publisher of Quartet Books). Asprey already had a little boutique in the Trump Tower on Fifth Avenue in New York when, in 1985, a major site at street level became available. Donald Trump was enthusiastic about Asprey's taking the space, but at that stage the firm looked warily on plans for expansion in the city, since the boutique had not been open long. Nevertheless, Naim Attallah managed to negotiate terms with Donald Trump that were good news for everyone involved. "Asprey now has the most prestigious site in the Trump Tower," he says happily.

Chairman John Asprey showed his appreciation of the efforts of his colleague and friend in a uniquely appropriate way. Aware of Naim's lifelong passion for lapis lazuli, he surprised him with a lapis lazuli egg. Reliving the moment, Naim Attallah says, "I saw this magnificent egg: it was from Afghanistan, the only place in the world where they have this dramatic blue lapis. You could never, ever find another!"

The anonymous gift of appreciation is imbued with the spark of mystery. Who could be unmoved by the gesture of the unknown admirer recalled by Doris Saatchi, renowned collector of modern art and London correspondent of Condé Nast's American *House and Garden*: "One day when I was coming out of the house to set off on the day's chores, I found one long-stemmed pink rose tucked into the handle of the door of my car. I don't know who left the rose for me, but I am cheered up every time I think of it. Thank you, whoever you are."

Rao Rajah Hanut Singh
to Julian Hipwood

Even in that toughest of field sports—the game of polo—there is a place for personal sentiment. Julian Hipwood, captain of England's Polo Team, rarely wears spurs on the field, yet for the past eight years he has always carried a pair in his polo bag. They were a gift from international polo player Rao Rajah Hanut Singh, Hipwood's hero and mentor. "I owe everything that I have achieved in polo to Singh," he says.

Singh first noticed Hipwood's exceptional promise when England's future captain was little more than a boy. The two had met by chance when they played together in the Cirencester Polo Team. The older player promptly invited Julian to play on his own team in England, offering him board and lodging, a mount, and pocket money. The offer taken, Singh supervised his protégé's progress from dawn till dusk. Hipwood recalls that the day began at five o'clock with a ride, followed by breakfast, after which "I had to go off and, for hours, do something called 'wooden horse'—practice on a life model of a polo pony." He played polo four times a week. "Life was one hundred percent polo," he says ruefully, remembering those days.

Later, when Hipwood played in India, Singh continued to shape his pupil's game through an inimitable mixture of criticism and anecdotes: "He would recount strange and funny fables about polo players and what happened to them, always with a moral." On the field, if Julian attempted a shot that Singh considered too difficult for him, his teacher would shout, "I am Rao Rajah, I can do these shots. You are a nobody." To Julian's chagrin, Singh never praised his game; he cannot recollect a single casual "Good shot!" ever escaping his coach's lips. Even when Hipwood went on to become a feted six-goal player in India, Singh seemed unimpressed with his former pupil's game. He gave no formal sign of recognition of the success of his tutorship until the day when, following a match in which Julian had played particularly well, he came up to him and announced, "Now I can say to you, 'Julian, you are a polo player.'"

In commemoration of this private graduation, the spurs were presented. Julian speaks with tenderness as well as a sense of pride about these spurs that he has won: "There is nothing special about the make, but they were *his*."

Along with the trophy, an unframed snapshot of Singh accompanies Julian on his travels. It shows the old boy on his mount, in his immaculate turnout, and with mallet held aloft, like a Crusader's staff, in perpetuity.

Julian Hipwood in a polo match

Comte and Comtesse
Chandon de Briailles

As vice-chairman of Moët-Hennessy, which has among its brands such champagnes as Dom Pérignon, Moët & Chandon, Mercier, and Ruinart, Comte Frédéric Chandon de Briailles is no stranger to compliments. He especially enjoys being congratulated, as he often is, on his delicious wine "Fred's Friends."

Frédéric Chandon himself first tasted the wine when, in 1976, he visited Domaine Chandon, the winery in the Napa Valley, at Yountville, that is an offspring of Moët & Chandon of Epernay, France. His colleagues

there, John Wright, director of Domaine Chandon, and Wright's aide, Michaela Rodeno, revealed that they had a surprise for him—"your own little *cuvée*, for *les amis de Fred.*" A pictorial label had been specially designed for the bottle, reproducing two saucy ladies from a drawing by Alphonse Mucha, the famous Czech exponent of Art Nouveau.

Humorously named and hospitably inspired, "Fred's Friends" is a still wine, a light Chardonnay. It is made in small quantities and is sold only at Domaine Chandon.

Drusilla Caffarelli
to Roberto Gucci

Roberto Gucci

There are occurrences in everyone's life that make it difficult not to believe in omens and portents, signs and symbols. Because of such an incident, Roberto Gucci, distinguished member of the Italian family that created the fashion empire bearing their name, attaches a special meaning to a certain pair of cuff links. These cuff links symbolize a chance happening that significantly affected the direction of his life.

As a young man of twenty-two, Roberto was attending a cocktail party in Rome when he noticed that one of his cuff links was missing. He looked high and low but failed to find it and gave up the search. Later in the evening a charming young woman who was holding the lost cuff link in her hand caught his attention; she had been wandering around looking for a likely owner.

"Is it yours?" asked Drusilla Caffarelli. Greatly relieved, Roberto answered, "Yes!"

The same charming young woman was at his side when, some years later, he said yes again—this time at the altar.

Gaston Menier
to David Hicks
and Lady Pamela Hicks

*David Hicks and
Lady Pamela Hicks*

A touch of mystery makes a fine prelude to a present, as British interior designer David Hicks and his wife, Lady Pamela Hicks, daughter of Lord Mountbatten, found. Out of the blue, they received a letter from Gaston Menier, of the French chocolate family, saying: "If you would care to call me in Paris, I have something interesting to give you."

"So," David continues the narrative, "we went to see the old gentleman, and he gave us this watercolor, painted by the last Czarina of Russia, Alexandra Feodorovna, who was my wife's great-aunt. Because of the family connection and our love of antiquities, M. Menier wanted us to have it. The painting is of the imperial yacht, the *Standardt*; the frame, in the form of a life belt, was made by the sailor who looked after the Czarevitch, the Czar's hemophilic son. Apparently young Alexis Nikolaievich never let the picture out of his sight, whether he was in the Kremlin in Moscow, the palace in St. Petersburg, or at sea on the yacht itself. We treasure it: it used to be his favorite possession, and now it is one of ours."

Herbert von Karajan
to Marc Bohan

The pursuit of perfection is an interest that can be a strong bond, and so it has proved in the case of two leaders in very different spheres, Herbert von Karajan and Marc Bohan. The Austrian conductor, who is musical director of the Berlin Philharmonic and director of the Salzburg Music Festivals, and the French couturier, who is chief designer of the House of Dior, are both known as perfectionists, and they have enjoyed a long friendship.

Bohan has been a frequent guest at the Salzburg home of von Karajan and his wife, Eliette, during the festivals. It was while visiting in 1983 that he received as a keepsake a signed and dated portrait photograph of von Karajan inscribed by him "A mon ami Marc."

This treasured portrait of the maestro, in which he is seen against a background of harps, prompts Bohan to acknowledge how much of his own understanding of music—especially the work of Gustav Mahler and Richard Strauss—he owes to Herbert von Karajan. As far as he is concerned, Bohan declares, "Their music belongs to him!"

Ray Stark
to Omar Sharif

People who live unsettled lives tend to be short-changed when it comes to presents, as film star Omar Sharif wryly points out. "I was always a nomad, always traveling and living in hotels. I never really stayed in one place for any length of time. And people knew that I was living in hotels so there was no use giving me things." Thus when producer Ray Stark, inspired by the success of *Funny Girl*, presented him with a group of original Toulouse-Lautrec posters, Sharif had to store them with an art dealer until he finally had his own flat in Paris.

The posters appeal to Sharif not only because he likes the work of Lautrec but also because they fit in with his simple, modern decor, or, as he puts it, "they go very well with my life-style." The association with *Funny Girl* and its star, Barbra Streisand, adds to the pleasure he takes in this gift. "*Funny Girl* was one of the most enjoyable films to make. I was used to making tiring films—out in the desert or up in the mountains, and this one was nice and comfortable. And it was Barbra's first film—she was really funny in it—and we had a ball."

Audrey Hepburn, inimitable screen heroine whose style has been imprinted on a whole generation, tells a story that, she says, "all real dog lovers can appreciate."

Robert Wolders
to Audrey Hepburn

"A special gift is often made so because of the special moment in which it is given. Like a drink of water in the desert, it might even mean survival.

"For many years I had had a little Jack Russell terrier called Jessy. She was born at home. She became my shadow. It was her gaiety and sweetness that started me off each day, and it was the warmth of her little body curled up at my feet that soothed me to sleep at night, whatever the trials and turmoil, the ups and downs, of the day had been.

"One day in Rome—I had to do some shopping—we were walking along the sidewalk and Jessy began to behave strangely. She had picked up some poison and was dead in twenty minutes.

"I nearly went out of my mind. I was inconsolable; my tears wouldn't stop. Weeks went by, and I was sick with misery.

"When I was in London to present a British Academy Award, through a friend we were given the name of Christopher Grievson, finder of the best pups in the world. It is he who found Penny, a tiny white Jack Russell with one brown ear and huge doelike eyes, and it was Robert Wolders, my sweet friend, who gave her to me.

"Penny crept into my arms and into my heart and with innate intelligence seemed to know exactly why she was there—to console me.

"She is so full of love and fun. I am never without her—a gift that not only gave me back my sanity but also my happiness—truly a Penny from Heaven!"

When Audrey Hepburn came to America to make the television movie *Love Among Thieves* (first aired in February 1987), Penny, then two-and-a-half years old, came with her, and was soon the pet of the entire crew of sixty; at times she even sat in the director's lap during the shooting of the film.

Lady de Havilland
to Olivia de Havilland

To Olivia de Havilland, the most precious object in her house in Paris is the silver christening cup of her heroic young cousin Geoffrey Raoul de Havilland (1910–1946).

Members of the de Havilland family grace the pages of the history of both science and the arts. In Britain Sir Geoffrey de Havilland (1882–1965), aircraft designer and manufacturer, was a pioneer in long-distance and commercial jet flying as well as military aviation. Across the Atlantic, the beautiful Olivia de Havilland made cinema history with Oscar-winning performances.

In 1942, during World War II, in which de Havilland planes such as the *Mosquito*, the *Vampire*, and the *Hornet* played an important part, Geoffrey Raoul de Havilland, eldest son and namesake of Sir Geoffrey, and chief test pilot of the company, came to Canada and the United States to test and demonstrate the Canadian-built *Mosquito*. He paid his cousin Olivia in Hollywood a surprise visit. It was their first meeting, and they took to each other at once. From then on, says Olivia, "It was hands across the sea." When Geoffrey returned to England this new and treasured friendship was carried on by correspondence. But it was all too brief, for on September 27, 1946, Geoffrey was killed while test-flying an experimental tailless high-speed jet aircraft, the DH 108, probably at a speed greater than had previously been attained by man.

Geoffrey's christening cup was given to Olivia by his mother, Lady de Havilland, a tribute and a memorial to a friendship tragically cut short.

Above, Geoffrey Raoul de Havilland
and Olivia de Havilland

Ben Stevenson
to Cleo Laine and John Dankworth

Cleo Laine

The spirit of friendship between British and American artists is very real to Ben Stevenson, artistic director of Houston Ballet since 1976 and winner of three international gold medals for choreography. Before coming to Houston he was co-director of the National Ballet in Washington, D.C.

In the mid-seventies, British singer Cleo Laine and her husband, jazz musician John Dankworth, heard that the main sponsor of the National Ballet was leaving Washington. They rallied to the cause and gave a benefit performance at the D.A.R. Constitution Hall in Washington.

To express his appreciation of their generous action, Stevenson presented his British friends with a symbol of the achievements of a British dancer he enormously admires: a pair of pink satin ballet slippers that had belonged to Dame Margot Fonteyn and that—to judge from the abundant scuff marks on the toes—had seen her through countless hours of dancing.

Set on a mount with the inscription "Love to Cleo Laine and John Dankworth from the dancers of the National Ballet: Shoes of Dame Margot Fonteyn" and dated October 30, 1974, the ballet slippers have danced their way from Britain to America and back again.

Lord Mountbatten
to Barbara Cartland

*Lord Mountbatten and
Barbara Cartland*

Barbara Cartland, whose romantic novels are best-sellers worldwide, singles out unhesitatingly as "the nicest present I've ever had" a token given her by Lord Mountbatten, an old friend and a personal hero. His gift was a black Labrador retriever (a nephew of his own beloved Kimberly); Miss Cartland named him Duke. She was profoundly touched by the gallantry of the gift, which all too soon acquired a special poignancy. "It was at Christmas in 1978 that Duke came to look after me. And then the following August Lord Louis was assassinated."

Duke was given to Miss Cartland in appreciation of her efforts to raise support for the United World Colleges, of which Lord Mountbatten was one of the founders and over which he presided from 1968 to 1978. To promote this cause, he and Miss Cartland collaborated on a novel, entitled—appropriately enough for a co-author who was Britain's First Sea Lord—*Love at the Helm*. Miss Cartland recalls that she told her colleague, "It will be easy. You write the naval part, I'll write the love part." And they did. The proceeds from the sale of the novel (published in England in 1980 and out of print except in the large-type edition) accrue to the Mountbatten Memorial Trust, which supports both the United World Colleges movement and technological research to benefit the disabled. With his loyal and gentle disposition, Duke symbolizes to Barbara Cartland the qualities she most admires. She reports, "Duke is a very good guard dog and a very good friend."

Dominique Benjamin
to Ben Kingsley

Ben Kingsley

When British classical actor Ben Kingsley, title star of the film *Gandhi*, was absorbed in playing the complex and demanding role of Othello in the Royal Shakespeare Company's production at Stratford on Avon in 1985 (September–November), the furthest thing from his mind was granting interviews. But he made an exception and did talk briefly with the French Canadian journalist Dominique Benjamin and even granted her request to photograph him in costume. The Stratford engagement was followed by a run at the Barbican Centre in London (January–March 1986), which aroused a phenomenally emotional response. During the last extraordinary week—

"as dramatic in the auditorium as it was onstage"—a cardboard tube mailed from Montreal was delivered to the stage door for Kingsley. When Ben finally took it home and wound down enough to open it, he burst into tears: Dominique Benjamin had so perfectly captured on canvas the Othello he had created that he could only think, "I am dreaming this!"

As an actor Kingsley is mindful of the ephemeral nature of his art and of actors' "battle to hold on to something tangible." Because of this gift, he says, "there is hanging on my wall something that defies the ephemeral."

Prime Minister Shimon Peres
to Lord Weidenfeld

A gift with unique personal and historic associations was presented to Lord Weidenfeld of the publishing firm of Weidenfeld & Nicolson on January 24, 1986, by Prime Minister Shimon Peres of Israel. The occasion itself was historic: in honor of Prime Minister Peres, Lord Weidenfeld had invited a group of some thirty distinguished writers, philosophers, and academics to join in an informal discussion over breakfast. For his host, the Prime Minister had brought with him from Jerusalem an ancient dagger that dates back to the days of King Ahab of Israel, who is the first king of Israel to be mentioned in Assyrian documents. "To receive such a beautiful and rare

object from Shimon Peres, whom I have known well ever since publishing his memoirs ten years ago," said Lord Weidenfeld, "was most touching and memorable."

Lord Weidenfeld has been the publisher of many world statesmen, among them General Charles de Gaulle, President Lyndon Johnson, Dr. Konrad Adenauer, Dr. Henry Kissinger, and Prime Ministers Harold Wilson and Edward Heath. Since he has many personal and professional ties to Israel (where he served as President Weizmann's adviser in 1949–50), he has also published the memoirs of Golda Meir, Moshe Dayan, Teddy Kollek, and General Yitzhak Rabin.

Jeremy Irons to Sinead Cusack

"Part gift, part cautionary tale," is the way Tony-winning actor Jeremy Irons describes a token that he presented to his wife, the accomplished actress Sinead Cusack, a leading player with the Royal Shakespeare Company and a member of the well-known Irish acting family. The object in question is a polychromed wood figure of a woman, probably dating from the seventeenth century. The actor found it in an antique shop on Lexington Avenue in New York during the time when he was playing there in *The Real Thing* and Sinead was playing in *Much Ado About Nothing* and *Cyrano de Bergerac*. He thinks it was originally a wall decoration in a ship.

Says Irons, with tongue in cheek: "I have always had a fictitious lover by the name of Flossie Fluepipe whom I hold over my wife. I thought it salutary for Sinead if Flossie did not remain a wholly imaginary character—

if we had a statue of her around the house. Flossie has a strange carefree quality that makes me laugh whenever I look at her. She is a little chipped, as all good women are; she has been about a bit. A bared breast is a generous gesture, and the flowers in her hair are a sign of a sort of generosity. She also reminds me of one of Canova's *Three Graces* in the Hermitage. She does not remind me of Sinead. One's fictitious mistress must be completely different from one's wife; it keeps the wife on her toes because she cannot hope to attain the qualities of the mistress. If Sinead sees me sitting there looking longingly at Flossie, she knows that she's in trouble."

Flossie was not given to mark an occasion. Irons confesses that when occasions come up he can never find anything, and when he buys something for a future occasion he can never restrain himself from giving it immediately. "In the main we aren't great gift givers to each other. Sinead gives me children, which is the greatest gift, and I give her the gift of my company and my conversation, which is indeed delightful especially in the early morning. I probably get the better end of that bargain!"

THE HUMOROUS GIFT

Above, Jeremy Irons and Sinead Cusack

One point is clear about presents that are given in a spirit of humor. They are usually much more fun for the giver than the receiver—which no doubt explains why the idea has lasted for such a long time.

There are almost as many different kinds of humorous presents as there are types of humor: whimsical, comical, farcical, black, erotic, satirical. In general, the giver of the humorous present seeks, as a first priority, to entertain and amuse, and, in the course of fulfilling this aim, to discover, devise, or dream up an idea outside the realm of the usual. It is an endeavor bristling with social dilemmas, since there is a fine line dividing the acceptable and the unacceptable. It must be admitted that few people enjoy a good joke on themselves—and this is true particularly in the gift-expecting context. However, presents with intent to amuse have in their favor that they make good stories to look back on in tranquillity.

Practical jokes are the mainstay of those who hope to wrap up a present that will evoke an appreciative laugh. Sometimes this will do the trick where other, more expensive or more conventional notions might fail. It seemed to offer a solution to Count and Countess von Schönburg-Glauchau, who, with Christmas 1980 in the offing, were pondering on what to give their new son-in-law; Prince Johannes Thurn und Taxis had married their daughter Gloria and taken her off to live in splendor in his fabulous castle in Regensburg. Gloria's sister, Maya (who later became Mrs. Mick Flick), says of that time, "We were not so rich. We couldn't buy a Cartier watch or a cow." Taking their cue from the Prince's love of practical jokes and his habit of setting delicious chocolates out on the tables at all times, the Schönburgs presented him with a box of chocolates. But they had put into these delicious-looking chocolates fillings of mock caviar and fish paste!

As a prank, this ploy lacked the bite of a caprice of the Prince's own that has passed into family lore. It is said that he once presented a woman friend whose great pride was a collection of rare fish with an addition to her aquarium. She turned to thank the Prince for his present and kissed him. When she looked back at the aquarium, only the newcomer was visible. The present was a piranha.

A practical joke can be a way of taking the sentimentality out of a corny situation. Such was certainly Warren Beatty's intention on an occasion recalled by Joan Collins, TV star extraordinaire. One day—it was three o'clock on a Saturday afternoon, and they had just finished lunch—Warren said that he was hungry for some chopped liver and added that he had gotten some the day before. Joan opened the refrigerator and took out the container. She opened it and said it smelled delicious. But not until, prodded by Warren, she had looked at it very carefully did she discover that stuck in the middle of the chopped liver was a gold ring encrusted with diamonds and pearls—an engagement ring. . . .

The notorious parsimony of John Paul Getty in the matter of personal remembrances encouraged two close and longtime friends to make a joke of it, albeit obliquely. When Margaret, Duchess of Argyll, as a present to Getty, gave him a party on the occasion of his eightieth birthday, she asked the band to play a specially composed song, the words of which parodied Cole Porter's memorable "You're the Top," with verses such as this: "You're the top, you're like Jack Benny, / You're the top, wouldn't waste a penny. . . ."

Another friend of Getty's who managed to have the last word on his Scrooginess was Lady Diana Cooper, the classic English beauty, actress, wit, writer, and wife of the British diplomat Duff Cooper. She was less surprised by Getty's gift to her of a front door for her house on Warwick Avenue in London than by the fact that he gave her a present at all—as can be read between the lines of the inscription on the plaque she put up: "This door was presented by J. P. Getty."

Getty himself almost seemed to enjoy his reputation for closeness. Lord Lambton, a friend of long standing, recalls: "He once gave me a curious present when he came to stay, shortly before his death, for Easter. He arrived with a loved companion after a long journey from Sutton [Sutton Place was Getty's residence in Surrey]. As he drove down the avenue he must have noticed the ground was covered in yellow daffodils. However, not to be discouraged, when he came into the house he presented me with a small bunch of wilting daffodils that he had picked in Surrey and brought all the way to Northumberland as a fitting Easter present. He may have seen an ill-mannered look of surprise flit across my face, for he said, his face crinkling into a lupine smile, 'I see you have got plenty on the drive, Tony, but now you will not have to pick them.' I thanked him heartily and accepted the gift with pleasure."

The wealth of a recipient is more difficult to poke fun at by way of a present than parsimony. However, it can be done. Patrick Lichfield, a leading British fashion photographer, presented his brother-in-law, the Duke of Westminster, who is said to be one of the richest landlords in the world, with a Monopoly board marked with the properties for which the Duke's Grosvenor Estate collects rent in real life. It included Grosvenor Square, Park Lane, Mayfair, and Belgravia, and although Lord Lichfield was unable to find any Grosvenor Estate–owned railway stations, he was able to fill in these spaces with foreign airports that the Duke uses when he inspects his properties overseas.

The best private jokes often show a straight face to the outside world. On a visit to Hollywood, Albert Einstein called on Charlie Chaplin. The eminent physicist wanted to know all about comedy and the movie business, while the world's most famous comedian was interested only in the Depression, socialism, and economics. The meeting went like a dream. After an hour the genius of the screen asked the genius who laid the foundations of modern physics for a photograph of himself. Einstein obliged, inscribing it "To Charles Chaplin, the great economist."

No one could call rock star Elton John's humorous present to his friend impresario Mel Bush half-baked, since it is based on a Walls pork pie, the most popular brand of its kind in Britain. Elton commissioned Cartier to reproduce a Walls pork pie in miniature in the form of a brooch. It was executed in 18-carat gold and was extraordinarily realistic, even to the gradations of shading that baking produces on a pie crust and a proper indented pie frill surrounding the top. Mel Bush's name was lettered on it in the style of the logo used on Walls wrapping paper. At £1,435, "it was a most expensive pork pie," as Dennis Gardner, head of design at Cartier commented.

A remark made in jest has been known to generate a present that is humorous only by virtue of its context. Ibiza-based Princess Smilja de Mihalovitch can vouch for this. The Princess, who operates in the fashion world on the Spanish island, is a keen golfer; her house faces on the first hole of the Golf Rocca Llisa, and on the green she wears a special golf watch with a green-centered face, the second hand designed as a golf ball. Because the watchband was showing wear, one day when her friend movie director Roman Polanski was going to Paris she asked him as a favor to take the watch with him and try to find a replacement for the band, adding playfully that if he couldn't come up with a match he could always take the watch to a jeweler's—say Cartier—and have the whole thing remade in gold and emeralds. Time passed, and the Princess forgot about the commission until a day when she was lunching with film star Ursula Andress at Brasserie Lipp in Paris, and to her surprise Roman Polanski joined them. "He tossed me," she recalls, "an untidily wrapped parcel. I opened it and found the exact watch that I had described in my facetious remark—a beautiful gold watch decorated with eight emeralds chosen to match exactly the green color of the face of the original watch. . . . Roman is the only person who could have done it: he has so much imagination and so strong a sense of friendship."

Black humor built into a gift perhaps enables people to come to terms with the unthinkable. Ringo Starr of the Beatles found a macabre way of exorcising the memory of a fearful car crash from which he and his new wife, Barbara Bach, narrowly escaped with their lives. He had two fragments of the shattered windshield of their Mercedes-Benz set in gold and made into twin brooches, one for Barbara and one for himself.

While visiting his friend Baron Ricky di Portanova in his villa in Acapulco, George Nicholson, of the renowned firm that produces Camper & Nicholsons yachts, was moved to dub him "the killer of flies," for at that time the area was plagued with the creatures. Watching his host ceaselessly thwacking the air around his head in a desperate attempt to outwit the winged insects, one day George remarked what Ricky really needed was a matched set of flyswatters from Asprey's. That this was no idle jest Ricky found out when, to his astonishment, he received the flyswatters exactly as specified—made by Asprey's of sterling silver, trimmed in gold. According to Ricky, "They are works of art, the most beautiful flyswatters in the world. They are far too lovely to use for killing flies."

These days the di Portanovas control the fly population through spraying, and the gift flyswatters are displayed at their house in Houston.

The Surrealists were past masters of practical jokes with a serious purpose. Salvador Dali, who pushed everything to its limits, applied his principles to gifts bestowed upon him. When the decorator Jean Michel Frank presented him with a pair of exquisite late-nineteenth-century chairs, he took one of them and removed its leather seat, replacing it with one made of chocolate. Then, under one leg he placed a Louis XV doorknob (thus precariously tilting it to the right), while another leg was made to repose in a glass of beer. Voilà: he had created the original Surrealist object.

The bohemian world of Paris in the early part of the century is the setting of a present with a history full of irony. Among the many artists of that period who were struggling with poverty was Modigliani. When he had first arrived in the capital and was subsisting on his parents' meager allowance, he had appeared quite a dandy. Indeed, he was affectionately known as "the aristocrat" around Montmartre. Once he was having a drink with the Chilean artist Manuel Ortiz de Zárate when the great Picasso strolled by. Ortiz de Zárate pointed out this celebrated figure to the young Modigliani, who remarked that the man might have some talent but dressed like a tramp. Some years later, when Picasso had risen to further heights and Modigliani had not yet gained recognition, the older artist decided to discard a worn

The Michelin Man portable tire pump

Spanish corduroy coat, weather-beaten and stiff as a suit of armor. He gave it to a friend (possibly the poet Guillaume Apollinaire), who subsequently donated it to the impecunious and now shabby young painter. Thus "the aristocrat" was reduced to wearing the castoffs of the Spanish "tramp." Actually, "Modi" was so pleased with the offering that he and the giver wrote out the history of the coat and gummed it to the inside lining.

Mistaken identity is as often a source of the comic situation in gift giving as in other human encounters. A cautionary conclusion could be drawn from an experience of the great Auguste Rodin. The famous French sculptor, together with his models and his assistants, was having lunch at his residence, the Villa des Brillants in Meudon, when a tin box arrived express from Greece. It immediately became a source of speculation. Caviar? Foie gras? An ancient figurine? Or even, as Rodin jokingly suggested, a bomb? This humorously intended suggestion was quickly taken up by the sculptor's women companions, who implored him not to touch the ominous object. Rodin was not of a suspicious nature, but he strongly believed in woman's intuition, so the tin box was buried deep at the end of the garden. A few days later a letter arrived from an old friend in Greece, inquiring as to whether Rodin had received the Hymettos honey he had sent, knowing as he did Rodin's passion for the Hellenic world.

The humor in caricature derives from distortion, hence the caricature is a daring gift. However, Adam Gimbel pulled it off nicely when he made a present of a caricature to Salvatore Ferragamo. The two men had become good friends through their business relations, Gimbel as president of the New York department store Saks Fifth Avenue and Ferragamo as one of Italy's leading shoe designers and the founder of the international Ferragamo fashion business. On one of Adam Gimbel's trips to Italy he visited the Ferragamos at their house in Fiesole, near Florence. Leonardo, Salvatore's son, remembers the occasion: "They were sitting in the garden and Gimbel... produced a notebook on which he sketched a caricature of the face of his friend Salvatore. He then gave him the drawing as a present." This particular humorous portrayal by a friend is treasured by the subject and his family.

Sometimes an epic achievement is most aptly commemorated by a lighthearted offering. It would be difficult to think of a more vivid symbol of Sir Terence Conran's acquisition of the Michelin Building on Sloane Street, a London landmark noted for its Art Nouveau decoration, than the unusual memento discovered by his wife, Lady Conran, in 1985 at a sale of memorabilia at Christie's and presented to him. Sir Terence is the creator of the chain of Habitat furnishing shops that has changed the buying tastes of the public. Caroline Conran is a noted writer on food and the author of cookbooks that have become classics.

The souvenir is a version of the Michelin Man, the mascot of the Michelin Tyre company, whose headquarters are in the Michelin Building. His proper likeness, composed of tiers of rotund car tires, adorns both the exterior and interior of the building. The rare ribald interpretation of the image is a portable tire pump. The memento is displayed in the London office of Sir Terence, who declares, "He is the best!"

Family jokes inspire the sort of presents that make up in sheer fun for what they may lack in monetary value. Thus Princess Maria Cristina de Bragança recalls a memento given to her by her husband, Miguel Berrocal, the well-known Spanish sculptor who lives in Verona:

"This is a story about a play on words. In the Italian language the word for small ruby and watertap is the same, *un rubinetto*. A ruby is *un rubino*. So for many years in our family it has been a custom to describe anyone who is loaded with rubies and jewels as having a lot of watertaps. One year I remarked to Miguel that I would like, as a present for my birthday, a small ruby. I received instead a watertap. He had bought a regular watertap, which he had polished himself, wrapped up, and then given to me. I kept it, but it has always reminded me that if you do not express your wishes clearly you may never get what you want for your birthday."

Every woman who marries an Englishman with a dog knows in her heart of hearts that she has an implacable rival. Qualified proof of this can be seen in the experience of the lovely Elizabeth Harris, daughter of Lord Ogmore, who was first married to Richard Harris. Elizabeth recalls that during her marriage to Rex Harrison, in the seventies, the actor had a basset hound named Homer to whom he was devoted. "I think Homer had been through a number of marriages and was a fairly chauvinistic animal. Homer really disliked women. He would wait until you had got dressed and then he would come and slobber all over you.... While Rex was writing his autobiography, *Act One, Scene One*, he was puzzling over whether the book should be dedicated to Homer or to me. It was touch and go, and when at last I was presented with a copy I was very much surprised to see that the book was dedicated to me."

However, the fact that the book contained a snapshot of the threesome captioned "Homer, Rex, and Elizabeth" prompted the last-named to remark, "Rex wouldn't give me top billing all the way!"

Rock Hudson
to Claudia Cardinale

Rock Hudson and
Claudia Cardinale
in A Fine Pair

Rock Hudson and Claudia Cardinale made two films together, but they had more than professional stardom in common. They were both individuals whose private lives as well as their performances on-screen were marked by sophistication and style. Both, in their separate ways, were interested in extracting enjoyment from living and both believed that life was too short for absolute conformity. They also shared a keen appreciation of the pleasures of the table. When Claudia Cardinale was living in Hollywood (where she had rented Elizabeth Taylor's house), Rock was there on most evenings, sampling the delicacies produced by her Italian cook.

In 1966 they were making the film *Blindfold*, which was shot in Hollywood and in Tampa, Florida. In one scene they appeared together in their underwear. When the filming of this episode was completed, Rock presented his leading lady with his shorts, inscribed with the word "Occupied," and various other humorous messages—an evocative reminder of a friendship that was tragically terminated by Rock's death, in 1985. Yet, as Rock would have wished, the garment moves Claudia to laughter, not tears: "It makes me laugh whenever I see it, because we were always laughing together."

Rudolf Nureyev
to Wayne Sleep

*Rudolf Nureyev
and Wayne Sleep
taking a bow*

Wayne Sleep, the classical ballet dancer who has now pirouetted into the realm of popular entertainment with his own company, DASH, owns a bittersweet memento given him by the Russian-born dance star Rudolf Nureyev. "Rudolf was the first person to put male dancers on the map at the Royal Ballet," says Sleep. "He managed to create many male solos and made dance in England much more exciting. He was very encouraging to me. When I joined the Royal Ballet Company (I was twelve), he gave me a good part in the Nutcracker."

It was in 1975 that Nureyev and Sleep were in London performing with the Royal Ballet at the Royal Opera House, Covent Garden. Nureyev was dancing by night and by day playing the lead in Ken Russell's film *Valentino.* "I was going to have the part of Nijinsky in the film because Rudolf wanted me to," recalls Sleep. However, Ken Russell let it be known that he had other plans for the role of Nijinsky. Shortly afterward, the star arrived at Covent Garden with a gift offered partly in jest, partly to make amends: a T-shirt with a picture of Rudolf as Valentino on it and signed "With love, Rudolf."

"My first feeling," Wayne admits, "was 'You can keep your stuffy T-shirt,' but then I saw how Rudolf had signed it. Although it was a joke, really, it is sweet to have."

Marcel Marceau

Phyllis Block
to Marcel Marceau

Marcel Marceau, who ordinarily deals with life's dilemmas wordlessly, through the art of mime—in which he reigns supreme in the world—also on occasion makes use of the written word.

He wrote a fable about a poor man who works as a clerk in an office and wants a bowler hat more than anything else in the world. Eventually he goes out and buys the nicest bowler hat he can find. One day he discovers that he cannot get the hat off his head: when he goes to the theater to see a Charlie Chaplin film, people yell at him because they can't see over his hat. At home he fights and fights with the hat, to no avail. Finally he has an operation to remove the hat and then he cuts the hat up, puts the pieces in a bag, and drowns the dismembered hat in the river. Happy to be rid of the bowler, he goes to bed. The next morning he goes outside and looks up at the sky. What does he see but an armada of thousands of bowler hats flying in formation toward him!

This fable inspired a New York member of Marceau's worldwide audience, Phyllis Block, to make him a present of a bowler hat safely contained in a cage.

Lady Muriel Richardson
to Birdie

Birdie, an Amazon parrot, had been a member of their household ever since Sir Ralph and Lady Muriel Richardson found him in a flea market in Spain. The parrot was singularly attached to the actor, who would always after returning home from the theater release his pet and spend an hour or so in play, exercise, and conversation (partially in Spanish) with it.

When, after Sir Ralph's death, in 1984, Lady Muriel moved to a smaller house, Birdie's routine—exercise in particular—became something of a problem. To the rescue came the Richardsons' theater friend Stanley Hall, a bird fancier and, according to Lady Muriel, "the greatest international wig maker and perfumer there ever was"; he offered Birdie a perch in his aviary at Ewhurst Green, in Sussex, which also provided a haven for Frevo, a Brazilian rain-forest tortoise given by Sir John Gielgud to Stanley Hall as a Christmas present.

To ensure that Birdie would feel at home in this new domain, Lady Muriel sent the parrot off with two of its favorite playthings, a toothbrush and a pipe that had belonged to Sir Ralph—souvenirs that would be coveted by any member of the great actor's host of fans.

Gianni Agnelli
to Baron Hans Heinrich
Thyssen-Bornemisza

One of the world's finest collections of European art in private hands belongs to Baron Hans Heinrich Thyssen-Bornemisza. It is housed in La Favorita, the Baron's villa on Lake Lugano in Switzerland, but it is enjoyed by people all over the world because of the Baron's generous lending policy. Sharing the wall space of the villa with masterpieces such as Balthus's *The Card Game*, to name only one, is a framed document from another realm of discourse—a check for one dollar made out to the Baron.

The provenance of this document is interesting. Gianni Agnelli, chairman of the board of directors of Fiat, invited the Baron to join the board of his holding company, IFINT. In order to serve on the board, the Baron had to buy a nominal amount of stock, and when IFINT declared a dividend, he received as a return on his nominal shareholding the nominal sum of one dollar. Thus it came about that Gianni Agnelli, one of Italy's industrial giants, presented to Heinrich Thyssen-Bornemisza, head of the world-class conglomerate that bears his name, a check for a single dollar. The irony is all the sharper in view of the longtime friendship of the two financiers, dating back to when they met as teenagers. "I consider it a gift," the Baron says of the check. "It is more expensive to cash than to keep!"

Above, Baron and Baroness Thyssen-Bornemisza

Sergio Galeotti
to Giorgio Armani

In his drawing room in Milan, world-renowned designer Giorgio Armani keeps a memento that he regards as "a most precious object, full of meaning." It is a ship's barometer in a briarwood and polished brass case, and it was given to him on his forty-ninth birthday, in 1983, by his close friend and business partner, Sergio Galeotti.

The gift of the barometer was one of the high points of an ongoing exchange of verbal sallies that the two friends engaged in throughout their fifteen-year partnership (ending only with Sergio's death, in 1985)—an exchange based on the contrast between Armani's famous frugality and Galeotti's famous openhandedness. They

made a game of it, Armani chiding Galeotti for his "indiscriminate generosity" and Galeotti twitting Armani on his "tightfistedness." It was in the spirit of the game that Galeotti presented Armani with the costly barometer; when Armani learned the price (12 million lire, a sum then close to eight thousand dollars) he apparently blanched. Galeotti had scored!

With the passage of time the humorous aspect of the treasured memento has given way to deeper meanings. On occasion Armani uses the case of the barometer as a repository for private thoughts that he has put in writing— "notions I can tell only to Sergio," he says.

Enrico Job
to Lina Wertmüller

One thing that the Italian trail-blazing writer-director
Lina Wertmüller will never have to worry about is
mislaying her eyeglasses—the white-rimmed eyeglasses
that are her signature prop. For this security she can thank
her husband, sculptor and scenic designer Enrico Job.
One Christmas he conceived of what he thought would be
an unforgettable present: he lavished upon Lina about five
thousand pairs of white-rimmed eyeglasses. As it turns
out, if Lina Wertmüller wishes to make a gesture to a
friend or give an admirer a token of her esteem, she is able
to present a pair of white-rimmed eyeglasses like her own,
and they have become much-sought-after souvenirs.

Queen Elizabeth the Queen Mother to the Prince and Princesse de Beauvau Craon

Aerial view of Château de Craon, Haroué

with us at our country place, Haroué, near Nancy.

"The day after the Queen Mother's arrival, my husband and I took her around the grounds. Going through the orchard, I told the Queen Mother that a few months after our marriage, an article had appeared in *Country Life* magazine that brought an unexpected reply

Queen Elizabeth the Queen Mother presented a gift to Prince and Princesse de Beauvau Craon, her host and hostess in France, that has become a tailpiece to a family legend. The de Beauvau Craons are one of the premier families of France; Château de Craon, in Haroué, an eighteenth-century castle designed by Germain Boffrand, is the great house of Lorraine.

The story of the gift is told by the Princesse de Beauvau, who, since the death of her husband in 1982, is very much involved in the preservation of French historical houses as president of the International Committee of the Demeure Historique (the association that covers the 2,000 privately owned castles of France) and who has recently joined the staff of Sotheby's:

"Queen Elizabeth the Queen Mother loves France and comes every year for a short visit. In 1979 she stayed

from a reader in Canada. The writer of the letter had recognized in the description of Haroué the place in which his grandfather had been keeper (*régisseur*) in the nineteenth century. He and the other grandchildren of the keeper had been brought up on the story of how their grandfather had helped Prince Charles de Beauvau Craon bury the family silver in the orchard in 1870, during the German advance. He asked, had we found the silver? No.

"The Queen Mother smiled silently. Three days later we accompanied her to her plane, which had just arrived from London to take her back to England. Out of the plane came a big brown box. 'I have been calling up Harrods for three days to find what I wanted,' said the Queen Mother, as she gave us the box. Eagerly we opened it, and there was the metal detector with which we are still searching for the treasure of Haroué."

David Niven, Jr., to Princess Esra Jah

Every family—and indeed every group with a lasting relationship—develops a highly personal vocabulary. Bywords and in-jokes become a language understood only by those who speak it. Just such a network of records and recollections grew up within a group of about six friends of which David Niven, Jr., and Princess Esra Jah (former wife of the then Nizam of Hyderabad) were part. Holidaying together yearly, traveling to many different corners of the world, these friends had many odd and comical experiences. "Wherever we went, some incident happened which either we laughed about or it was a secret just between us," says Princess Esra, and she explains that for each of these incidents there is a code word or phrase that has taken on a private significance.

The Princess describes her good friend David, the son of the famous actor, and now a film producer, as "very, very amusing." Certainly "amusing" is the word for his Christmas gift to her of six silver matchbox covers by Asprey, each one engraved with a date and the appropriate words. These inscriptions mean nothing to outsiders, but they cause the insiders to "fall about, laughing," as Princess Esra puts it.

Pierre Bergé
to Yves Saint Laurent

Yves Saint Laurent says he is a dog person. By this he means that he is never without his dog, Moujik, night or day.

"When traveling I always take him with me, and when I can't, as to England, I don't go.

"We are both set in our ways, with our foibles, but most important of all we have the same tastes. He likes certain materials—don't laugh, but the sound of taffeta being unrolled sends him into a frenzy. Moujik has even modeled at one of my collections, walking down the runway with a girl dressed in black and white, just like him.

"So when my friend Pierre Bergé gave me his portrait, painted by Andy Warhol, for Christmas in 1986, I was both overjoyed and moved, because the painting was of Moujik but also because it was by Andy, who had done my portrait fifteen years before.

"After those days Andy and I rarely saw each other, but I knew everything about him, about his career and his work, his movies and his books. My admiration for him never diminished.

"So let's not play with words and get straight to the point: Moujik by Andy was the best Christmas present I could have dreamed of."

Above, Pierre Bergé and Yves Saint Laurent

THE
GIFT OF
FRIENDSHIP

Friendship is the maker and shaper of presents. From earliest times, individuals have conveyed goodwill through giving—a custom that finds its apotheosis in friendship. Mementos, tokens, remembrances strengthen the ties of comradeship and seal bonds between good companions. Undoubtedly one of the keen pleasures of friendship derives from the ability—based on intimate understanding of the recipient's tastes and predilections—to bestow the ideal gift. A true friend is someone who knows what you would die for, wrapped or unwrapped.

A public tribute to a friend is a gift with a special dimension. The thirty-year-long friendship of Audrey Hepburn and Hubert de Givenchy was signalized by just such a gesture on a gala occasion in 1982. Hepburn flew from Switzerland to attend the opening of the major retrospective exhibition *Givenchy: Thirty Years* held at New York's Fashion Institute of Technology (May 10–October 2). Although the actress had made clear that she would attend in a private capacity and would not participate in the formalities, she surprised everyone by delivering what Givenchy recalls as "the most beautiful, beautiful emotional speech. . . . It was impossible for me to say one thing! I just kissed Audrey." Afterward, Hepburn presented the designer with the handwritten text of her tribute, "Thirty Years of Givenchy," a prose poem of friendship and praise, in which she said of the man who had designed most of her film wardrobe, "Since always, he has cloaked me in his talent."

That people never outgrow the charm of being surprised, Doris Brynner, former wife of Yul Brynner, had well in mind when she was planning a present for Stavros Niarchos, the Greek shipping magnate. She ordered a customized Fiat—a doorless *cinquecento* (the 1100) with a light and pretty wickerwork interior and sportive canvas awning—to be dispatched to the tycoon at Monte Carlo. When the vehicle arrived unannounced on his doorstep he thought there must have been some mistake, and he was all the more delighted to learn that it was intended for him. The ingenious giver had neatly gauged his liking for useful playthings: the advantage of the model was that, being lightweight, it could easily be taken aboard a boat for a cruise and would provide a handy runabout for guests disembarking at ports of call.

Any friend of Salvador Dali's can expect the unexpected in the way of presents. The artist liked to be seen in the company of a pet ocelot that belonged to his secretary. The animal was admired by, among others, Prince Juan Carlos of Spain, who remarked that he would like to own one. Dali, known as a lover of the species, was occasionally presented with an ocelot. The next time this occurred, he decided to give the animal to the Prince.

Hubert de Givenchy and Audrey Hepburn

However, the security detail at the palace in Madrid thought otherwise, and the artist's offering was politely rejected. Meanwhile, the ocelot had the run of the Hotel Meurice in Paris, where Dali was residing. A visit from fellow artist Miguel Berrocal of Verona gave Dali his chance. Aware of Berrocal's fondness for strange and baroque possessions, he announced grandly, "Here is your present, Juan Carlos's ocelot." The animal traveled with Berrocal by car to Verona, where it was taken to the veterinary surgeon to have its claws removed. We are told that "the ocelot lived happily at Berrocal's house—and there were no robberies."

There is no surer guide to selecting a welcome present than the aim of building up a friend's collection. Princess Ira von Furstenberg's collection of some forty porcelain cups has been augmented by gifts from the designer Antoine Chenevière, who is her partner. Together they run Tzigany, the well-known antique shop of Geneva and London.

The cups, dating from the eighteenth and nineteenth centuries, are decorated with mottoes, emblems, and devices, and also depictions of animals. The Princess, whose collection began with a few cups given her by her mother, comments, "They are all different in style and shape. I like seeing the collection getting bigger and bigger, but mainly for amusement's sake. They are not jewels; a cup is something you can enjoy every day. I love these cups." Antoine Chenevière picks up suitable additions to the collection at auctions and at dealers'. "What is particularly entertaining are the inscriptions. Ira, being Austrian, is partial to porcelain. The bulk of the collection is Austrian, and these little cups with their varied decorations in a sense represent Ira's history."

Gifts given by great artists may cast light on the private side of a rare imagination. Picasso always knew what to give Gertrude Stein to delight her. The writer has recalled that she had been very fond of little pigs since her days in Assisi, when she often used to see an old woman leading, instead of a goat, a little pig, decorated with a red ribbon, up and down the hills. Picasso made and gave Stein some charming drawings of the Prodigal Son among the pigs.

Gertrude Stein's most widely quoted aphorism, "A rose is a rose is a rose," owed its airing to the instincts of her long-time companion, Alice B. Toklas. It was Toklas who singled out the line in a manuscript by the author, and put it to use as a device—on letter paper, table linen, and anywhere else that she was allowed to—a true present of its kind. Later, Stein herself made similar use of the words: some plates that she had made specially by a local

Princess Ira von Furstenberg's porcelain cups

potter in the regional yellow clay of the Savoy, where she was living, for her friend and editor Carl Van Vechten were decorated with the rose maxim around the border and the words "To Carl" in the center.

Composer Giacomo Puccini and conductor Arturo Toscanini were the closest of friends as well as colleagues (Toscanini was responsible for the premieres of Puccini's *La Bohème* and other works.) As a mark of respect and admiration Puccini gave the maestro and his wife, Carla, a pair of magnificent five-branched silver candelabras. For the maestro's daughter Wally, when she was ten years old, in 1911, the composer inscribed on the corner of a record album a line from the libretto of his opera *La Fanciulla del West* ("The Girl of the Golden West"), *Il mio bimbo è grande e piccino* ("My baby is both big and tiny")—accompanied by the music. The record album on which the composer penned these words and notes has long since been set in a silver frame and preserved for posterity. The candelabras are now among the prized possessions of the maestro's two daughters, Wally and Wanda; each has one of the pair.

On the completion of *The Leopard* (1963), in which Claudia Cardinale played the role of the flawlessly beautiful heroine, against a backdrop of nineteenth-century opulence, the Italian film star received a gift that was entirely in keeping with the mise en scène. The celebrated director, Luchino Visconti—an international creative force in the world of the cinema and the lyric theater—made a gesture that to Cardinale epitomizes one of the qualities that made up his greatness—his sensitivity. Visconti presented her with an antique *carnet de bal*; it came wrapped in an Indian shawl in blue and gold. Another gift from Visconti was a purse, received on the completion of the film called, in English, *Conversation Piece*, in 1974. Cardinale remembers Visconti with profound admiration as "a prince, one of the last princes. . . . He *was* the Leopard."

The friendship between the two British theater knights Sir Alec Guinness and Sir Ralph Richardson, an engaging item of stage lore, yielded a number of presents in addition to many anecdotes. However, according to Sir Alec, the giving was lopsided. Sir Ralph, "always generous to a fault," presented him with a finely bound set of the plays of Sheridan, an exquisite malacca cane with a rhinoceros-horn handle, and a beautifully carved walking stick. "All I ever gave him, I think, was a classic work on parrots, when he bought José [later named Birdie] in Spain, and a white azalea, on his seventieth birthday." This minimalist version is expanded by Lady Richardson, Sir Ralph's widow: the "classic work on parrots" was a first edition of W. T. Greene's three-volume *Parrots in*

Candelabras and inscribed record album given by Puccini to the Toscaninis

*Gifts from Luchino Visconti
to Claudia Cardinale*

*Luchino Visconti directing
a scene with Claudia Cardinale*

Captivity published by George Bell and Sons in London in 1884–87 and containing many exceptionally fine colorplates. The books were cherished by both the Richardsons.

Among the many gifts from friends that Margaret, Duchess of Argyll, renowned English beauty and socialite, has received, she singles out for its historic overtones a remembrance from Haile Selassie, the last emperor of Ethiopia. When the Duchess was visiting Africa in the company of her son in 1972, she spent the last lap of the journey in Ethiopia, where she was the personal guest of the Emperor and his daughters. Her host presented the Duchess with a collection of silver Coptic crosses, representing various regions or provinces of Ethiopia, mounted in a silver frame. Displayed in her Park Lane apartment, these unusual crosses are reminders of a memorable journey and of a national leader whose hospitality was far more felicitous than his political fortunes.

"A tree makes a wonderful present. It suggests that you are likely to be around for a few more weeks at least." Beatrix Miller was prompted to make this observation in recalling an occasion when, as editor-in-chief of British *Vogue*, she was entertaining Leo Lerman, then features editor of American *Vogue*, at lunch at her newly acquired country retreat in Wiltshire. The day was unusually warm and sunny, and her guest expressed a desire to sit in the garden. However, she found she had no parasol and had to improvise a substitute. Shortly afterward there arrived from her friend Leo Lerman the gift of a young willow-leaf pear tree, a species that when grown is a good source of shade.

Friends and acquaintances of British artist Donald Evans are often given fanciful drawings for imaginary postage stamps that reflect in some way their interests and predilections. One friend, Kaffe Fassett, noted British textile designer and author of the successful manual *Glorious Knitting*, admires speckled birds' eggs, so Evans sent him a postcard with an individual series of postage stamps depicting this favorite theme. The drawings later inspired the textile designer to make a needlepoint of the subject.

Needlepoint is a medium that can make the gift of friendship wonderfully personal. Capucine, the French film star who first came to public attention when she modeled Givenchy's couture collection in the fifties, gave to the designer two cushions she had worked in needlepoint depicting his country manor, Le Jonchet, in Romilly-sur-Seine. "The idea is to have two versions, Le Jonchet in summer and Le Jonchet in winter. I think this is wonderful."

Presents of pets extend the ties of friendship, as French novelist Françoise Sagan would surely agree. The writer received from Paris dress designer Peggy Roche a fox terrier that has become her inseparable companion. Her dog's name is a reference to Françoise's one-time passion for gambling: the cry that issues from players of baccarat in the casino when they stake all—Banco!— is the call the little fox terrier answers to.

The gift that is presented by a group of friends has the weight of numbers. A particularly elegant offering was devised by guests at Baron Alexis de Redé's Oriental ball at the Hôtel Lambert in Paris in 1967. They presented their host with a beautifully designed album, produced in India, portraying costumes worn at the ball, details of the decor, and some of the more opulent features of the entertainment, such as riders of elephants, garbed in Indian robes. The drawings were done by Alexandre and Catherine Serebriakoff. Among those who subscribed to the remembrance were Mme. Jean-Claud Abreu, Brigitte Bardot, the Duchess de Cardaval, Salvador Dali, James Douglas, Baronne de Günzburg, Mme. Konrad Henkel, Serge Lifar, Mme. Arturo Lopez-Willshaw, Prince Rubert Loewenstein, Aileen Mehle (Suzy), Mme. Vincente Minnelli, Mme. Atenor Patino, Vicomtesse de Ribes, Arnaud de Rosnay, Baron David de Rothschild, Baron and Baronne Guy de Rothschild, Mme. Pierre Schlumberger, Baronne Gérard de Waldner.

Personal and international friendship were intermingled in a gift presented by a group of friends to West German publisher Frieder Burda. A friend and supporter of Axel Springer (1912–1985), the outspoken anti-Nazi, pro-Israel, humanitarian head of a vast West German publishing empire, who had a deep love for the city of Jerusalem, Frieder Burda has carried on Springer's work. In May 1986 Burda took a group of fifteen leading West German entrepreneurs on a tour of Israel. The special reason for the trip was the laying of the cornerstone of a project for the restoration of the Lion's Gate in the wall of the Old City of Jerusalem. On this occasion (May 4), Burda received from Jerusalem's mayor, Teddy Kollek, a formal citation officially expressing his appreciation of Burda's efforts in behalf of the city. He also received, from his fifteen grateful friends, a silver box decorated with a gold-engraved map of Israel with rubies marking many of the historic places on their itinerary.

There is no such thing as a typical friend's present, fortunately. However, many of us will go along with the definition of a basis for friendship's bounty formulated, with sublime indifference to spelling, by the British artist Francis Bacon: "Champagne for real friends. Real pain for cham friends."

Opposite top, Donald Evans's postage stamps with Kaffe Fassett's speckled birds' eggs

Opposite below, Needlepoint cushions worked by Capucine for Givenchy

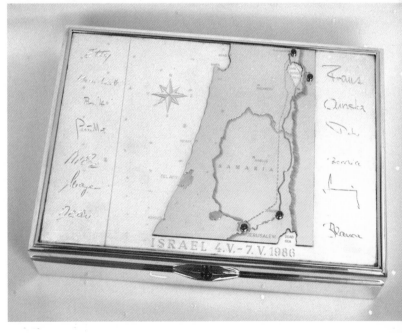

Above top, Françoise Sagan's fox terrier, Banco (left), with his mother, Lulu

Above, Silver box with gold-engraved map of Israel given to Frieder Burda

Salvador Dali
to Gabrielle "Coco" Chanel

Salvador Dali, the Surrealist whose works are notable for their weirdly imaginative combinations of images, painted for his friend Gabrielle Chanel a picture that is the essence of simplicity. It portrays a solitary ear of wheat.

Dali said of Chanel, in his autobiography, "She could speak of France as no one else could; she loved it body and soul. . . ." One of the things she loved, and Dali knew this, was wheat. "For her it was a lucky symbol," recollects Pierre Ceyleron of the House of Chanel. "Every year she would bring a sheaf of cut wheat from the country, and she would buy anything with wheat."

The designer's fondness for wheat derived perhaps from memories of childhood in the farmlands of the Cévennes: a good harvest would cheer the farmers through the winter. Whatever the origin of her predilection, Chanel surrounded herself with the color and forms of wheat. She rarely—if ever—designed a collection without using wheaten shades. She acquired many objects with the wheat motif for her home; among these curiosities are a wooden baker's shop sign carved with a sheaf of wheat and an arrangement of *faux* stems of the grain made of painted metal.

Dali's little painting still hangs in the designer's daytime apartment in the House of Chanel, on rue Cambon, where she would spend her working hours and often entertained her friends.

Above, Chanel in a photograph by Horst

Comte and Comtesse
René de Chambrun
to Ambassador and Mrs. Joe M. Rodgers

United States Ambassador to France Joe M. Rodgers and his wife, Honey, were charmed by the Comte and Comtesse René de Chambrun from the moment they met, in Paris in 1985. The Comte is a direct descendant of Lafayette, and his mother, an American, was Clara Longworth. The Comte and Comtesse, both in their eighties, are indeed an impressive couple. They live in the Château La Grange, which was Lafayette's house, and are the custodians of this de facto private museum containing the finest private collection of American Revolutionary papers. The Comte, President of the French branch of the Sons of the American Revolution, a member of the New York Bar since 1934 and of the Paris Bar since 1935, has been president of Baccarat Crystal since 1960. The Comtesse is the daughter of former Premier of France Pierre Laval.

Ambassador and Mrs. Rodgers found they had much in common with René and Josée de Chambrun, who have many American connections. One day they entertained the Comte and Comtesse at lunch and afterward, in the game room, showed the movie *The Spirit of St. Louis* (the Comte had been on the airfield the night Lindbergh landed). Their guests admired the Ambassador's huge collection of elephants and in the course of the conversation were shown what the Ambassador thought was "the smallest elephant in the world."

The next day there was delivered to the Rodgerses an elaborate package containing, within a chocolate shell, a perfect little ivory elephant that could be seen only with a magnifying glass. Ambassador Rodgers, whose connection with elephants began at his alma mater, the University of Alabama (mascot: the elephant), and was reinforced when he was Finance Chairman of the Republican National Committee (1979–81), believes that as a result of this beau geste by the de Chambruns he does own the smallest elephant in the world.

Richard Burton
and
Elizabeth Taylor
to Peter Ustinov

Peter Ustinov

"We all got on rather well," says actor, producer, director, novelist, and playwright Peter Ustinov, referring to Elizabeth Taylor, Richard Burton, and himself. All three appeared in the film *Hammersmith Is Out*, which was made on location in Mexico in 1972.

So well did they get on that the Burtons were moved to present Peter with a painting by Mexico's leading contemporary artist, Rufino Tamayo. They reserved two pictures and asked him to choose one; the other one would be theirs. Ustinov, though he was worried that he would choose the painting that the Burtons wanted, accepted the offer with pleasure.

The Tamayo painting hangs in the drawing room of Ustinov's house in Switzerland in the company of other treasured objects, among them a sculpture by his son Igor and his famous collection of hippopotamuses.

A gift from Peter Ustinov to Elizabeth Taylor is described by him simply as "an inadequate jewel."

Princesse Ghislaine de Polignac
to Baron Alexis de Redé

The inscription, in Latin, reads: *Alexis stinthia genuit ornavit Ghislainia*, which could be translated "For Alexis, the ostrich laid the egg, Ghislainia made the decoration."

In pursuit of her idea for a gift to her friend Baron Alexis de Redé—a fantasy re-creation in miniature of the seventeenth-century Hôtel Lambert, where the Baron has lived for many years—Princesse Ghislaine de Polignac, brilliant hostess and center of a cosmopolitan circle in Paris, took her cue from a show of Fabergé's fabulous jeweled Easter eggs. As the inscription indicates, she chose an ostrich egg to represent the house. *L'Oeuf d'Hôtel Lambert* reproduces many of the architectural details of the original, carried out in rare materials. French windows are framed in vermeil. The egg balances on ormolu dolphins, emblems of the Hôtel's location beside the river Seine.

The inside—a re-creation of the famous Galerie d'Hercule of the Hôtel Lambert—is as wondrous as the outside. The Hôtel was built on plans by Louis Le Vau, and the Galerie was decorated by Charles Le Brun (both architect and artist were later to set their mark on the splendors of Versailles). When the little windows are open and the interior is illuminated by candlelight, "you have the whole of the Galerie d'Hercule as it appeared in the past," says the Princesse.

The Russian artist Alexandre Serebriakoff produced beautiful sketches of the exterior and interior of the egg and gave final shape to the Princesse's idea. The bronze work was done by a remarkable firm of French craftsmen founded three hundred years ago. The Princesse recalls, "The *bronziers* worked with the same tools as their ancestors used in the seventeenth century."

The presentation of *L'Oeuf d'Hôtel Lambert* was a complete surprise. The Princesse savors the remembrance: "The Baron thought the idea highly amusing and the execution sensational."

*Princesse Ghislaine de Polignac
and Baron Alexis de Redé*

Halston
to Elsa Peretti

As if it were a living flower, Elsa Peretti keeps her coral rose in a vase. A gift from her friend and colleague Halston, to her it *is* living, in the sense that it grows in fascination, more and more. To begin with, this distinguished award-winning designer of jewelry, whose work Tiffany's is proud to lay exclusive claim to, loves coral because "it means for me—Italy!" And as a designer she knows that the amount of coral required for the carving of the rose "is very difficult to find now." More

important, Peretti is moved that Halston bought the pin—a hatpin—in Naples intending to give it to his mother but gave it to her. Peretti and Halston met while vacationing at the resort of Fire Island, New York, and worked closely together in the seventies. The hatpin is oddly appropriate coming from Halston, who began his notable career in millinery (he designed the famous pillbox that Jacqueline Kennedy wore at the 1961 inauguration).

Pierre Cardin
to André Oliver

*Pierre Cardin and
André Oliver*

The job interview that André Oliver had with Pierre Cardin was, as Oliver remembers it (after some thirty-five years), brief and to the point: "I said I was looking for a job, and he said, 'Okay, come!'"

At the time, Cardin was just beginning to be well known, having designed a very important costume for the famous 1951 masked ball given by Charles de Beistegui at the Palazzo Labia in Venice. Oliver, a lad of twenty, was just out of design school.

It seems as if the durability of the long association of Cardin, head of a fashion empire, and his co-designer and collaborator, André Oliver, was predicted by a gift that Cardin presented to Oliver in 1966—a rare early-seventeenth-century pair of mandarin ducks on a single base—for in Chinese iconography the mandarin duck is the symbol of fidelity. The pair of ducks is fashioned of pewter and gold (the small waterfowl was named the mandarin duck by Westerners in China because its bright, colorful plumage resembled the dress of the imperial mandarins). These ducks have been treasured by Oliver for over twenty years for both their beauty and their symbolism.

John Barrymore to Anthony Quinn

The last years of John Barrymore's life were plagued by drink and debt. Among the impoverished star's few remaining possessions was a finely wrought and engraved English suit of armor. He had worn the armor in his role as Shakespeare's Richard III, one of his most celebrated interpretations. The gift of this noble suit of armor was John Barrymore's valediction to his protégé, Anthony Quinn.

The beginning of the friendship that prompted the gesture has elements of the high drama that both actors were at home in on the stage. Quinn recounts that he first met Barrymore, his ideal of an actor, when, at the age of nineteen, he was playing the role of a man in his mid-sixties that had been written with Barrymore in mind but had been turned down by him. One night Barrymore himself was in the audience and came backstage to meet his impersonator. "He was astonished to find 'a kid' standing before him," recalls Quinn with obvious glee, which the passage of time has not diminished.

The two became close friends. "He was the most brilliant man I ever met," says Quinn. "I grew into a kind of adopted son. I always loved him. . . . He didn't believe in love, didn't consider himself worthy of being loved." Quinn remained on intimate terms with Barrymore throughout his life. When illness made transfusions necessary, Quinn discloses, "I kept him alive with my blood."

As Barrymore lay dying, he said to Quinn, "I have nothing to give you except my suit of armor. . . ." Then he produced a sheet of paper on which he had inscribed these lines:

> Tony, when an old bullfighter retires, he hands his preferred novillero his sword—I am handing you the armor I wore in Richard III.
> May it bring you the luck it brought me—and, watch the treacherous winds of time.

The suit of armor may be too small for Quinn to don, but it is an enduring and haunting reminder of the great actor who, as Quinn puts it, "set the course of my own star."

Prince Glebe Eristoff
to Jean Castel

As the convivial proprietor and lively personality behind the private club in Paris that bears his name, Jean Castel has inspired in his circle a high degree of esteem and affection. This is reflected in the splendid collection of presents that has been bestowed on him over the years by the members of Castel. Among his most treasured objects are those that relate to boats and the sea. A memento that is displayed in his private dining room, where he entertains his close friends, is a meticulous model of a vintage ship.

Jean Castel has been a keen sailor since he was a boy of twelve, a passion that resulted in his competing in the yachting event in the Olympics in 1948, a year when the Games were held in London. He still keeps a boat and enters it in the America's Cup race. A longtime member of Castel, Prince Glebe Eristoff knew of Jean Castel's liking for the sea and its craft, and presented him with this model, which had previously been in the gallery in St.-Germain-des-Prés, on the Left Bank, that the Russian nobleman had at one time owned.

Silvano Malta and Karl Lagerfeld to Anna Piaggi

Two favorite presents of Anna Piaggi's are inextricably linked, because one is a drawing of the other. The first is an original Fortuny dress, given to her in about 1967 by her friend the fashion designer Silvano Malta. A brilliant fashion editor and arbiter of taste and design, Anna Piaggi welcomed this addition to her collection of over a thousand costumes—the raw materials of her inventive and original style: "Silvano found the dress one Sunday morning. It was in a flea market in Rome, the famous Porta Portese, with some Hawaiian shirts and cost about a thousand lire. It still had all the original amber buttons, and I wore it to death." In fact, her irreverent treatment of the dress shocked her friend and fellow collector of Fortuny, Tina Chow. Anna would roll it up as a scarf and when it got torn, wear it "all gloriously broken."

But although she loves the dress as a thing of the moment and refuses to treat it as a museum piece, it in effect became one when, in 1977, the renowned designer Karl Lagerfeld, who acknowledges Anna as his muse, drew her wearing the dress. Their special "graphic relationship," as Anna calls it, began when he first sketched Anna's head on one of his cards in a Chinese restaurant in Paris in 1973, and he has continued to sketch her and many of her clothes. She would arrive in France to stay with him accompanied by eight or ten trunks, the Fortuny dress curled up in the corner of one of them. The dress is preserved for posterity in the 1977 drawing, labeled by Karl "Fortuny Punk," in *Lagerfeld's Sketchbook: Karl Lagerfeld's Illustrated Journal of Anna Piaggi* (London and New York, 1986).

Eschew evil and
do good

Cole Porter
to Claudette Colbert

Delightful, ageless Claudette Colbert loves to reminisce about composer Cole Porter—"a divine person, and a genius." In her apartment in New York she treasures a Battersea enamel box and a small French painting that he left to her in his will—"two lovely little things." They evoke many memories.

"I admired Cole more than I can say, and we were good friends. It seems to me that I knew him forever. . . . One lovely night we all went to a special showing at MGM of the musical version of *The Philadelphia Story* [*High Society*], for which he had written the music. He was so worried, and couldn't believe how marvelous it was. Afterward we went back to his house. Alan Lerner and Fritz Loewe were there, and because Cole had never seen *My Fair Lady* on the stage, Alan sang the whole score while Fritz played it. Cole was in seventh heaven.

"The last time I saw Cole was in New York at his apartment at the Waldorf Towers. We had dinner, just the two of us, and recalled times like that wonderful evening. And we talked about the two little old ladies in Peru, Indiana, his home town, who made wonderful fudge. He evidently had a standing order with them, and because I loved fudge he used to send me fudge from Peru about three times a year. . . .

"How wonderful he was, and what fun he was to be with. I have been very blessed."

Above, Claudette Colbert
with a cutout of herself as Cleopatra

Françoise Callier
to Kenzo

Kenzo, the first Japanese designer to make Paris look East, is a confirmed Parisian. But his favorite present—a collage of holiday photographs made for him by his friend Françoise Callier—reminds him of yet another corner of

the globe. Françoise, a friend for whom Kenzo always has time in his hectic life, is part of the group of people he usually goes on holiday with. They have been to such places as Kenya, Turkey, and Japan. The collage comprises photographs taken by Françoise during their 1984 Christmas vacation on a sailing boat in the Grenadines.

"I love gifts that are a complete surprise, as this was," Kenzo confesses. "And it was made with such love and humor. It continues to give me enormous pleasure, not just because of the actual memories it holds but because it enables me to dream of all the holidays still to come."

Above, Kenzo

Alfred de Cabrol
to Comte Guy de Brantes
and Comtesse Marina de Brantes

Anyone who has ever given a really successful party must envy Guy de Brantes, Director General of Hermès International, and his wife, Marina, the gift that they received the morning after their first big anniversary party. Observing the custom followed in Holland, Marina's native land, they invited all their friends and all the children to an Alice-in-Wonderland costume dinner party at their town house in New York to celebrate their 12½-year (halfway to 25) anniversary—called "copper" by the Dutch. One of the guests, Alfred de Cabrol, an Air

France executive in New York and an amateur painter whose works have been exhibited at the Wally Findlay Galleries, after leaving the party, went right home and worked all night to complete a painting of the party that, according to Marina, "is better than a photo." With his "fantastic photographic memory," de Cabrol recorded Guy as the March Hare, Marina as Alice, the children as various cards, their grandmother as the Queen of Hearts, their grandfather as the Mad Hatter, and many friends.

Everyone can be recognized, and the Comte and Comtesse have a strong sentimental attachment to this painting for its capacity to summon up remembrance of the party itself and of their friends.

A strong sense of history is a governing force in the life of Prince Pierre d'Arenberg, as well it might be, since the d'Arenbergs are an old European family first recorded A.D. 495 and based in France for the last two hundred years. Especially meaningful to the Prince, therefore, are two bronze portrait busts by sculptor Bichette Givaudan; one of these was a gift to him, and the other was a gift to his father, Prince Charles d'Arenberg, who died when Pierre was seven years old. There are at least twenty years between these two works, the later one executed in 1982.

Bichette Givaudan
to Prince Pierre d'Arenberg

Prince Pierre d'Arenberg

The story is an unusual one. The sculptor and Prince Charles were great friends and often went skiing together. During this time Bichette volunteered to make a bust of Charles in bronze. When it was completed, she presented him with the sculptured portrait.

Twenty years later, when the sculptor and her husband, Georges Revay, were guests of Prince Pierre at a shooting party, she offered to do a portrait bust of her host. Once more her offer was accepted.

"And I think that's the most wonderful present," says the Prince. "She gave her time—two hours a day for three months is a lot of time—and she gave her talent. And now I have this bronze bust that faces my father's bust in my library in the country." The work on the bust was done in the artist's studio in Paris. It was her main work of the year and was exhibited in the Grand Palais. Givaudan has made portrait busts of many notables, among them Giscard d'Estaing.

In giving the shooting party at the d'Arenberg country house (two hours south of Paris) the Prince, who lives in London, was keeping up a tradition established by his father and grandfather. Aware that he was born to privilege, Pierre d'Arenberg feels duty-bound to maintain tradition but also to bring it forward. This aim is eloquently symbolized by the two bronze portrait heads representing two generations.

183

Jean Cocteau
to Jean-Paul Belmondo

One day in 1961 the French poet, novelist, playwright, critic, visual artist, and filmmaker Jean Cocteau found himself on the same air flight as the French actor Jean-Paul Belmondo. It happened that Cocteau had previously tried to get Belmondo to work with him on his play *Beauty and the Beast* but was unsuccessful because Belmondo was already booked for a film. They had originally been introduced to each other by French film star Jean Marais, Cocteau's close friend.

During the flight the two men found much to talk about. They discussed boxing, a sport they both followed avidly. Cocteau had helped a boxer who was down on his luck work toward a comeback and a successful bid for the world championship. Belmondo had practiced the sport in his youth and had even dreamed of entering the ring professionally.

Apparently the conversation delighted Cocteau and he was moved to express his thoughts graphically. He drew a head-and-shoulders portrait of a young man and presented it to Belmondo. Inscribed "To Belmondo the Friend" it was signed and dated February 23, 1961.

Belmondo was greatly touched by this very personal act of recognition from so eminent an artist, and has given the drawing pride of place in his residence in Paris.

Above, Jean Cocteau photographed by Jean Howard

Count Etienne de Monpezat and Baron Alexis de Redé to Baronne Marie-Hélène de Rothschild

Amid all the works of art, bibelots, trophies, and treasures of the fabled domain presided over by the gracious Marie-Hélène de Rothschild, often called the Queen of Paris, the Baronne does not hesitate to single out an especially cherished gift. "It is my favorite object, that I find very moving" are her words for a stone roundel of the head of a woman given to her at Christmas in 1972 by the Rothschilds' good friend Count Etienne de Monpezat. The style of this late-antique relief sculpture, with its intricately modeled surfaces and sharp contrasts of light and shade, is typical of the art of the late ancient world

(from the second half of the third century to the first half of the sixth). "The head has such presence," says the Baronne; "it possesses the power of poetry."

Placed close to the roundel in a stately salon of the Rothschild mansion, the famous Hôtel Lambert, is an iridescent box in the form of a butterfly, wrought in enamel, gold, and diamonds in the late eighteenth century. A gift from Baron Alexis de Redé for the Baronne's birthday in 1976, the butterfly box alludes to one of her many hobbies. Baronne Marie-Hélène collects butterflies; she loves them and says, "The word itself is so beautiful in all languages!"

Above, Baronne Marie-Hélène de Rothschild

Hardy Amies

An eighteenth-century chair that stands by a bedroom window in the Gloucestershire house of Hardy Amies, British couturier who holds the Royal Warrant for H.M. the Queen, tells an interesting story, the hero of which is the late John Fowler, partner in Colefax & Fowler, London's leading firm of interior decorators.

Hardy Amies affirms that Fowler was "a tremendous influence on me. He taught me about antiques and about the ways of doing and using a room—about a whole way of life." The chair is a single instance of Fowler's infallible taste and his persistence. Originally it belonged to a

mutual friend of Amies and Fowler. As Amies recalls, "John insisted on reminding our very good friend that the chair was wrongly upholstered. But the friend would reply that he liked it that way, and in any event couldn't be bothered to make a change. Eventually our friend died, bequeathing the piece to John, who immediately had it reupholstered. The effect was absolutely splendid."

When John Fowler, died in 1977, Hardy, to his astonishment and pleasure, inherited the chair. He said, "Thanks to John, I am now the proud possessor of a very good, very unusual chair."

Hospitality is a gift without attributes: it has no shape or color, it cannot be seen or touched, yet its preciousness cannot be denied. To the beautiful, sensitive Italian actress Valentina Cortese, the hospitality of stage, opera, and film director Franco Zeffirelli is "the symbol of our friendship." Since they met, twenty-seven years ago, when Valentina was working with the Italian filmmaker Luchino Visconti, they have had a close, sister-brother

Valentina Cortese

relationship. Valentina numbers among her favorite films *Brother Sun, Sister Moon,* which she played in under Zeffirelli's direction in 1973. "I love Franco," says Valentina. "I call him my little brother and he calls me his little sister. He has told me that every time I go to Rome, I must come and stay with him in his wonderful house. If I am in Rome for only a day he insists that I pack my bags, leave my hotel, and move into his house. It makes me feel that I share Franco's home and life. . . . In my own house, in Milan, too, there are signs of Franco's generosity, like my beautiful bisque *Portrait of a Lady.*"

George Hoyningen-Huene
to Horst

Horst has not only a legendary name in photography but
also some fascinating memories and mementos,
many of them evoking the luminescent Paris of the
thirties. Above all, Horst remembers, while a student of
architecture with Le Corbusier, meeting photographer
George Hoyningen-Huene, who used him as a model
and became his inspiration and mentor. In their circle at
this time were such figures as Jean Cocteau, Man Ray,
Gertrude Stein, Chanel, and Christian Bérard. Horst,
who had started photographing in Paris for American
Vogue in 1931 (he was paid $3.50 for his first job), helped
Bérard, a painter, get work at French *Vogue* as a fashion
illustrator.

When, about 1933–34, Hoyningen-Huene had to go
to Hollywood to do portraits of the stars for *Vanity Fair*,
he asked Bérard to paint a portrait of Horst while he was
gone. Horst remembers eight or ten sessions of posing,
seated on Bérard's bed, with its yellow-and-white cover, in
the artist's tiny hotel room in Paris. When Hoyningen-
Huene returned from Hollywood, he was critical of the
portrait and summarily gave it to the sitter—to whom it
means a great deal because of his feeling for the donor.
Horst has another work by Bérard—a drawing (dated
about 1933) of Chanel, whom he first met in 1935–36. It
amuses him to recall that she said of his first photograph of
her, "It is a nice photograph of the dress but it is not me."
To this he replied, "How can it be? I do not know you,"
her answer to which was an invitation to dinner. After that
Chanel expressed her esteem for Horst and his work
through many gifts, among them a half-moon clock. To
Horst, Chanel remains "one of the nicest women I have
ever met in my life."

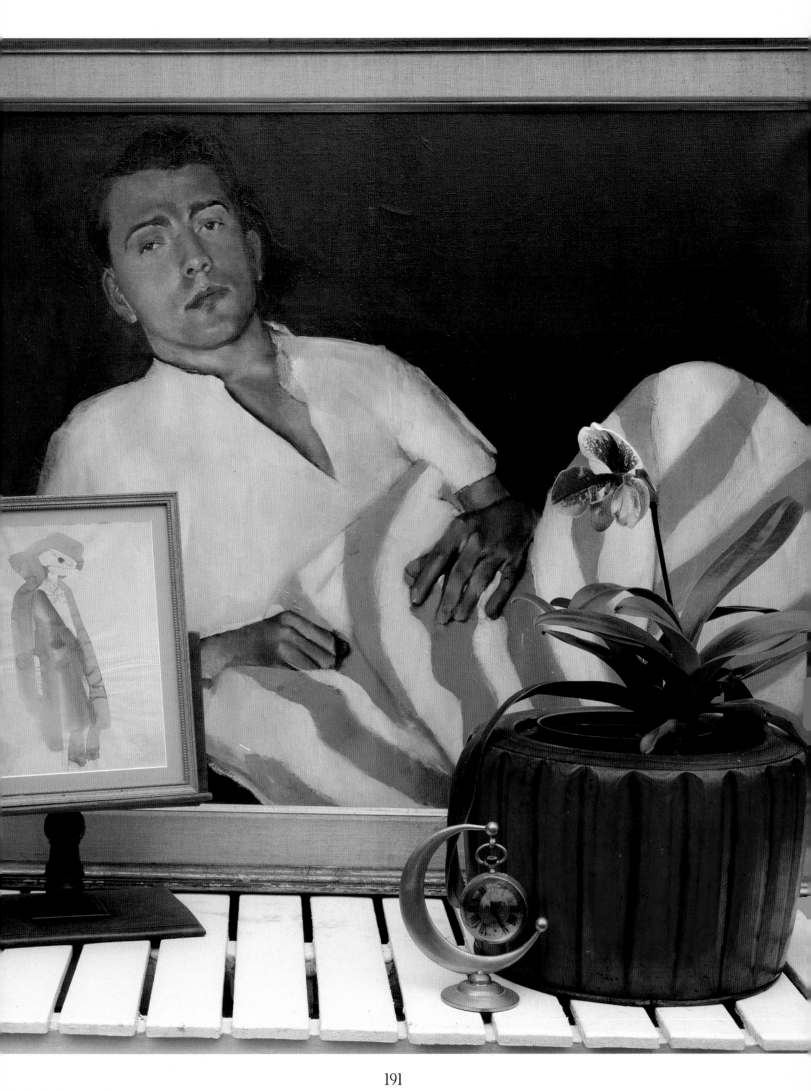

Marion Lawrence to Norman Parkinson

Internationally known photographer Norman Parkinson first encountered his "best-ever present" in the house of his good friend Alexander "Sandy" Perry Osborne II. He first met Sandy through Marion Lawrence, who had invited him to a house party at Castle Rock, in Garrison-on-Hudson.

Sandy was an all-round sportsman, but his real winter love was sledding, recalls Parkinson. "Each snowy day in winter he would check in with a sledding update: 'Deep snow, good frost, hard track. . . . Be here this weekend.'" The track was the winding drive, over a mile long, that climbed 400 feet from the main road to the house. Flexible Flyers would make their private Cresta Run at breakneck speed in two minutes. For the race Sandy would always wear his raccoon coat—a gargantuan garment that fascinated Parkinson. "Sandy would invariably start last. Halfway down, roaring with laughter, the raccoon coat would come racing through."

After Sandy died, ending a courageous twenty-year battle with cancer, Marion, aware of Parkinson's love for the coat, said to him, "Take it in memory of your friend."

Georges and Claude Pompidou to Jacques and Bernadette Chirac

A fifteenth-century weathercock that probably began its career atop a church tower in Paris has seen a lot of history. It became historic itself when Georges Pompidou, during his term as Prime Minister of France, found it, on one of his walks, in an antique shop and installed it in the official prime-ministerial residence in the Hôtel Matignon. There, *chez* Georges and Claude Pompidou, the weathercock was much admired by their young friends Jacques and Bernadette Chirac (M. Chirac was then secretary of state for economy and finance). When, in 1968, M. Pompidou left office as prime minister, and the Pompidous left the Hôtel Matignon, they presented the antique weathercock to the Chiracs.

Since then the weathercock has followed the Chiracs in all their official life. Because M. Chirac is both prime minister and mayor of Paris, he and his family divide their time between the Hôtel Matignon and the Hôtel de Ville (the official mayoral residence), where the weathercock adorns their private apartment. Although this keepsake becomes ever more historic, to the Chiracs it has, above all, a sentimental value because of their affection and admiration for Georges and Claude Pompidou.

Jo Lombardo
to Zandra Rhodes

When British fashion designer Zandra Rhodes talks about her creative process, the word serendipity is not used, but the principle is surely in her mind: "Oh, everything that comes my way is really like an inspiration!" One happy accident that sparked a whole series of prints and designs featuring the shell motif occurred when she was visiting her friends Jo Lombardo and Donna Malcé at their house in the Adirondacks. "At a garage sale we came across a basket with a lid all covered with shells and Jo bought it for

me and he added some glittering stones. I brought the basket back to London, where it sat in my small bathroom for ages. Then I suddenly started to draw seashells." The ensuing collection of fabrics and designs, launched about 1973, has forever linked the name of the designer with the shapes and colors of the seashell.

Zandra says she is very lucky in her friends, and she draws the moral: "A lot of gifts you can't put a value on at all. You can't always work out why a gift sparks you off."

Above, Zandra Rhodes

*Sir Cecil Beaton and
Sir Roy Strong*

A pen-and-ink drawing given to Sir Roy Strong, director of the Victoria and Albert Museum, by the artist, Sir Cecil Beaton, British photographer and designer, is loaded with memories of mutual regard.

The drawing, which portrays the terrace at Reddish House, Beaton's beloved Wiltshire retreat, is all the more remarkable for having been sketched after the artist suffered a massive stroke, in 1974; he had learned to draw, paint, write, and take photographs with his left hand.

Sir Roy recalls that he fell under Beaton's spell when as a teenager he had seen his set and costume designs for the production of Pinero's play *The Second Mrs. Tanqueray* at the Theatre Royal, Haymarket, 1950. "After the years of grayness, when everything was utilitarian, there was a sudden glimpse of beautiful spectacle and elegance" is how Sir Roy describes his reaction.

Beaton remained one of Roy Strong's great heroes, and when, at the youthful age of thirty-one, Strong was appointed head of the National Portrait Gallery in London (1967), among his first moves was organizing a retrospective of the photographer's work—the first major photographic show in a national collection—which made Beaton a semi-national figure. At the same time, says Sir Roy, "Cecil, a great setter of style, introduced me to everybody who was anybody. . . . He was one of the few originals I have known, and a great influence on me." Sir Roy also likes to recall Beaton's generosity with the contents of his marvelous garden and conservatory at Reddish: "Our house is full of cuttings of Cecil's geraniums, and Cecil's rosemary is in our garden."

William S. Paley
to François Catroux

In the Paris apartment of François Catroux, international interior designer, and his wife, Betty, is a memento proving that holiday memorabilia can gain in meaning with the passage of time. Frequent house-guests of CBS founder William S. Paley and his wife, the Catrouxs delighted in the company and hospitality of the Paleys during a succession of winter breaks in Nassau. Speaking of the late Barbara Paley, a luminary among a generation of distinguished hostesses, François Catroux recalls: "Babe was a beauty who made an art of pleasing her friends. Every imaginable civilized comfort was provided at the house." He remembers with particular pleasure her custom of supplying guests' rooms with a selection of the best of newly published novels and biographies. Good food was another bond between guest and hostess, willing listeners to each other. The Paleys had a great French chef whose delicious four-star dishes François Catroux has not forgotten.

During one holiday, when Babe Paley was trying her hand at sculpture, she asked François to sit for her. He agreed and posed for about an hour a day for two weeks, until she completed a portrait bust.

After Babe's death, in 1978, Bill Paley presented the bust to François Catroux. Observing the likeness, François is still amazed by the artist's understanding of his character. "It is my real face," he says.

*François Catroux
and Babe Paley*

Michel Guy
to Andrée Putman

The story of Andrée Putman's clock has all the ingredients of a fairy tale—a magic spell, a long search, a glamorous hero, and a happy ending. One day early in a career as an interior decorator that has led her to the top of the profession, she fell under the spell of "a magical object" in the window at Balenciaga's—a clock—that kept her transfixed for twenty minutes. The eight-foot-high clock was traditional, almost provincial in form, but its outside, of etched mirror, was "all about grace."

"That clock grows and grows in my memory... I see it in the window of one of the most important antique dealers, an impossible place. Eventually I see it in a film, and this magic object continues to grow and grow and has so much charm and power over me. Then, in 1963, I design an apartment of a house in St. Tropez for Michel Guy [Secretary of State for Culture, 1974–76], who happens to be one of my best friends for thirty years—not as a job but as fun. And Guy knows and has a very nice relationship with the impossible antique dealer....

"No one calls me, no one tells me anything, and the clock arrives at my house and I think I am dreaming, because it was almost eighteen years between the day when the clock was delivered to my place and the day I saw it in the window at Balenciaga's!"

Above, Andrée Putman

Fulco di Verdura to Tom Parr

Tom Parr, a director of Colefax & Fowler, the London firm of interior decorators world famous for grand English country house style, loves animals and has been collecting animals in art for years. Of his many porcelain animals, his favorites are a monkey and a rabbit made in China in the eighteenth century for the European market. Both came from the Palazzo Verdura in Palermo, Sicily, the ancestral home of Parr's good friend and traveling companion Fulco di Verdura, who gave them to him in 1974, a year before he died. These porcelains are quite rare, but Parr discovered in his travels with Verdura that many Sicilian noble families had wonderful collections of them.

Verdura was a man of many talents and had an extraordinary life, working in Paris with Chanel, in Hollywood, and in London. His skill as a painter is evident in a small gouache portraying the elegant sitting room of Parr's flat in Eaton Square, London. Verdura painted this while immobilized for three months after a car accident. Parr sets great store by the little painting and the porcelain animals (especially the monkey, which he finds very amusing). These are tangible reminders of Verdura, for whom he cherishes a lasting admiration: "He would describe himself—rightly—as *La Petite Larousse roulante*, in other words, a dictionary on wheels. His breadth of knowledge was incredible, and he saw everything from an unusual point of view."

Friends to Erté

The celebrated Russian-born costume designer and illustrator named Romain de Tirtoff and known as Erté (the French pronunciation of his initials), is the possessor of a remarkable collection of signatures, compiled over five decades.

The signatures are inscribed on the back wall of the bar in the artist's studio on the rue de Gutenberg in Paris, and they record all the friends, colleagues, and visitors who have come to his studio over the years. The names radiate from the words Chez Erté, boldly spelled out in metal studs arranged so as to form a witty self-caricature of the artist's face. The panel opens up to reveal a goblet-shaped recess equipped with glass shelves to

hold glasses and bottles.

The earliest signature on the panel is the paw print of Micmac, the artist's cat, dated 1936. Other signatories soon followed, among them Elsa Schiaparelli, the Paris-based Italian couturiere (1937), Prince Felix Yusupov, in whose palace Rasputin was assassinated in 1916, and the Prince's wife, Princess Irena.

The caricature on the signature wall is probably not entered in the log that Erté has kept of his drawings, which number 18,929. Doubtless this enormous figure does not include, either, the artist's first dress design, drawn when he was six—an evening gown for his mother, which she then made and wore.

Erté

Francesco Cirincione
to Gianni Versace

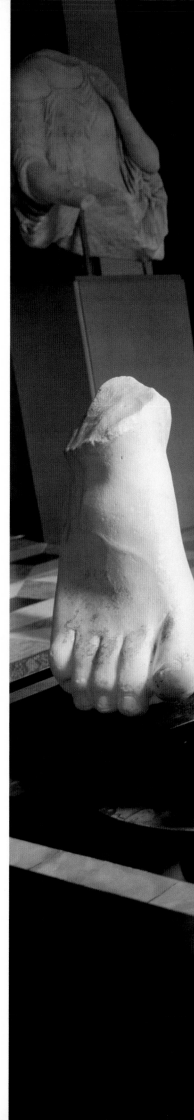

An unexpected gesture of generosity from a virtual stranger brought Gianni Versace, the Italian fashion designer based in Milan, the gift of a classical figurine that is one of his treasures.

"I was born in the south of Italy. My playground was a Greek temple near the beach. I am in love with classical shapes. One day in the window of an antique dealer in Rome I spotted a beautiful statuette. It had something unique—the spirit of ancient Greece in all its glory. Breathless, I asked the price (I wasn't exactly rolling in gold at the time). The dealer said he was sorry but there was a prior option on the piece. My dismay caused him to suggest that I leave my card, just in case.

"For weeks, each time I was in Rome I would go out of my way to pass by the shop and look lovingly at the statuette in the window. One day it was gone. I felt as if I had been punched in the stomach.

"The next day a parcel was delivered to me. It contained the statuette, with a note: 'Please accept this gift from a fellow lover of fine art.' I treasure it to this day. A symbol of the power of desire, it reigns above all the other pieces I have since collected."

The generous fellow lover of fine art was antique dealer Francesco Cirincione of Rome.

Above, Gianni Versace

Comtesse
Jacqueline de Ribes

The Marquis de Cuevas
to Jacqueline de Ribes

A ballet impresario in the grand tradition, the Marquis de Cuevas found a dramatic way to express his appreciation to the Comtesse de Ribes. He gave the elegant Parisienne, a fashion leader and designer—whom he named godmother of the Grand Ballet du Marquis de Cuevas in the last years of his company—a set of jewelry that had belonged to Sarah Bernhardt. The famed tragedienne had worn the jewelry when playing the role of the fabled Egyptian queen in Sardou and Moreau's drama *Cléopâtre*, which opened in Paris in 1890.

"Sarah Bernhardt's acting was acclaimed by the public, and critics found her extraordinary in this new

THE
GIFT OF
LARGESSE

part," comments Jacqueline de Ribes. Turning from
history to the recent past, she recalls wearing Bernhardt's
flamboyant jewelry at a fancy-dress dinner party during
a weekend at Ferrières (the château of the Baron and
Baronne Guy de Rothschild) at which Georges Pompidou
and Audrey Hepburn were fellow guests.

   "This unusual present," adds the Comtesse (whose
regal profile has been likened to that of an Egyptian
queen), "is an interesting and moving keepsake of a true
Maecenas and an exceptional man, no longer with us,
who used to call me, with affection and humor, his
'Pharaoh.'"

The gift of largesse draws on the universal love of the grand gesture. By definition it is memorable and tends to embody one or more of the coveted superlatives: most rare, most thoughtful, most beautiful, richest, best. Whatever the exact form of the offering, it helps to change the mundane order of things.

An elephant surely fits into the category of the grand remembrance. All manner of depictions of the beast figure in the records of present giving: jolly, cuddly, valuable, quaint, precious, to name some. However, few of us in the Western world can, like the aristocratic French d'Arenbergs, boast of having among our private spoils the gift of a live elephant; in the annals of that family presents of three live pachyderms are recorded. Prince Pierre d'Arenberg recalls that his grandmother Princess Pierre d'Arenberg, known as Maggie, was presented with an elephant by the Francophile Maharajah of Karputhala at the turn of the century (his palatial residence was built along the lines of French palaces such as Fontainebleau and Versailles). The Princess kept her trophy in the stables at 20, rue de la Ville L'Evêque, one of the four family houses in Paris. The Prince's mother, whose maiden name was Margaret Bedford, maintained the tradition. She was given an elephant by a Europe-loving Indian prince in the early 1960s. Prince Pierre remembers that his mother once "got all dressed up to go to a party and took the elephant with her." His sister Muffie, likewise, was presented with a diminutive elephant to which she became greatly attached. "The saddest day of her life was when that elephant was sent to a zoo," relates the Prince, who is elephantless.

An inspired act of largesse was the promise of Henry Goldman, founder of Goldman, Sachs, to the twelve-year-old musical prodigy Yehudi Menuhin that he would buy him any violin in the world that he wanted. The promised violin, a Stradivarius, was a glorious reminder to its player of an aesthete and a man of courage: Goldman was a collector of note who lost his sight in his declining years. Sir Yehudi played the instrument for many years, parting with it only in the 1980s, when, as he gratefully recalls, it helped him buy his handsome London house.

Sheer whim has been responsible for some of the most exceptional indulgences. The Yusupov family of Russia possessed land and mineral wealth and other assets on a scale that exceeded even the resources of the Czars (four palaces in St. Petersburg, three in Moscow, thirty-seven estates scattered across Russia). Prince Felix Yusupov, who was sole heir to this fabulous fortune, has recorded that his father gave his mother on one of her birthdays the highest mountain in the Crimea. What she did with it is not part of history.

Astonishment and largesse often go hand in hand, as in the tale told by Lord Lambton, the British writer and former politician, of "the most surprising present I was ever given." Around 1953, when he was in party politics, he went to a dinner given by a Major Renwick to celebrate the winning by one of his constituents of the Waterloo Cup, a greyhound racing trophy. "Major Renwick lived in the middle of the Northumberland Dales, which in those days were far remoter than they are now, and ruled a little kingdom with benevolent authority. He was a popular and generous man and all the personalities of the Dales were there and looking at him in a happy mood after the excellent dinner he provided.

"Suddenly to my amazement he turned to me and said, 'I now have an announcement to make, which is that I am giving our member of Parliament a candelabra which once belonged to my family.'

"At that moment the door opened and four men came staggering in carrying a silver candelabra nearly four feet high, which was placed in front of me. Quite overwhelmed with embarrassment, I said a few words through the silver spokes of the candelabra; they were greeted with polite applause, and then Major Renwick went back to his greyhounds and the affair was not mentioned again."

The largesse of nature that endowed Enrico Caruso with a voice unmatched for sweetness and power was equaled by the Italian tenor's personal generosity. Shortly after his recovery from throat surgery, Caruso and his wife visited a New York jeweler's in search of a present for his doctor's wife. While they were there, Dorothy spotted something that she wanted—a platinum chain for a watch that she had been given by her husband. Caruso remonstrated, "Doro, darling, I haven't sung all winter, I've just paid the doctors...."

Half an hour later, after they had left the shop, the singer produced from within his voluminous overcoat a package, which when opened revealed a yard-long chain of diamonds "because it is the first time that you ask me for something," he said. Then, handing his wife another box, he remarked, "I give you this because you ask with such sweetness." Inside was a ring set with a perfect black pearl.

Gambling casinos, legendary fount of good luck and ill, have inspired many memorable presents. Sir Basil Zaharoff, the munitions king of Europe, who was knighted for his services to the Allies during World War I, traveled frequently on the Orient Express. One night he took the part of a newly wed young woman who was being mistreated by her husband, a member of European royalty. The rescuer fell in love with his protégée, and

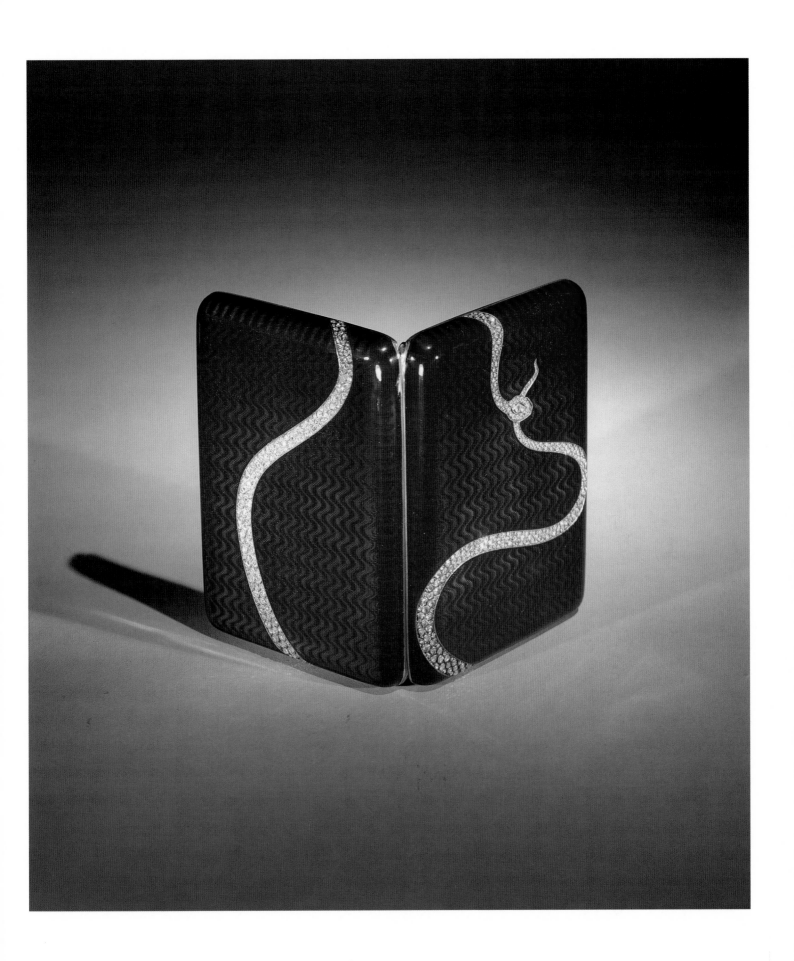

Fabergé cigarette case
given to Edward VII by Alice Keppel

they lived together for many years. Eventually, they were able to be married, within a week of Zaharoff's death, in 1936. Sir Basil gave his wife—a modest gift in those times—the Casino in Monte Carlo.

Even the smallest items having to do with gambling tend to take on the dimensions of largesse. French jewelry designer Jean Schlumberger made a copy of the "shoe" used in dealing cards in baccarat for his client Greek shipowner Aristotle Onassis. The artifact, which resembled an old-fashioned sugar scoop, held decks of cards so they could be dealt from the front, one by one. Onassis, who controlled the gambling at Monte Carlo at that time, commissioned the shoe as a present for his friend the Fiat head Gianni Agnelli because he was such a good customer. The piece was designed by Schlumberger in ebony, enhanced with ivory lozenges held in place by

Elton John wearing Cartier sunglasses

crosses of gold. The handle was of gold. The designer's biographer notes, "Both Onassis and Agnelli were delighted with the $15,000 shoe that worked just as well as an ordinary one."

A lavish way of sending compliments to the chef occurred to American film stars Douglas Fairbanks, Sr., and Mary Pickford when they were on their honeymoon in Italy in the 1920s. It seems that they had greatly enjoyed their choice of fettuccine at Alfredo's restaurant, on the Piazza Augusto Imperatore in Milan. The house specialty had been created originally by the proprietor in order to please his wife, who was pregnant at the time with their son—the father of the teller of this tale. She had asked if he would prepare a dish for her that was a little different from their normal fare. He made a plate of fettuccine using the freshest butter and the finest Parmesan cheese. The dish was so successful that it eventually found its way onto the restaurant menu as fettuccine Alfredo. When the American newlyweds returned home, they sent as a remembrance to Alfredo a solid-gold spoon and fork—the implements used to toss pasta, inscribed "To Alfredo, the King of Noodles," with their initials and the date, 1927. Since then, whenever VIPs come here to dine, their pasta is dressed with the gold spoon and fork. Among those thus served have been General Eisenhower, Clark Gable, President Kennedy, Robert Kennedy, President Reagan, and Frank Sinatra.

Money has nothing to do with some gestures of largesse; indeed the manner in which a memento is given contributes immeasurably to its sentimental content. When ballerina Natalia Makarova was presented with the *London Standard* award for ballet by the Princess of Wales at the London Coliseum in 1985, the dancer immediately returned the compliment by saying to the Princess, "All the flowers I have received tonight are yours." In turn, the Princess knelt down on the stage, picked up a small bouquet from among those that had been showered on Makarova and, in a gesture of homage, put it into her hands.

Finding appropriate offerings for members of the royal family to present to their hosts on far-flung foreign tours is the subject of much thought at Buckingham Palace. As in all present giving, it is difficult to gauge exactly what will give a frisson of pleasure to the recipient. A story about the young Queen Elizabeth centers on her first visit to the Kingdom of Nepal. The Deputy Master of the Household at the time, Lord Patrick Plunket, was a dedicated audiophile and as such he decided to provide a singularly sophisticated stereo system as the Queen's gift to the King of Nepal. Duly equipped, the Queen set off on the arduous journey by plane, train, and elephant. When the Queen returned to Britain, Lord Plunket eagerly awaited news of how the chosen present had been received. The Queen's apocryphal reply was, "Oh yes, they did like it—but they don't have any electricity over there, you know."

The rubric "largesse" would almost seem to have been invented to cover some incidents revolving around Elton John. On his birthday in 1986 the famous rock singer received from his friend Alain Perrin, president of Cartier International, a specially designed and inscribed Cartier moon watch with a sapphire and diamond face and strap. This elegant gift marked Elton's thirty-ninth birthday; it also reflected the age-old sentiment "A friend in need is a friend indeed."

That is what Elton proved himself to be when on March 23, 1983, he was a guest at a big bash held in Port El Kanthoui in Tunisia to launch Cartier's new line of sunglasses. About 600 people were flown there for dinner from all over Europe, and the chefs and provisions were imported from Paris. Perrin's wife, Marie Thérèse, had spent six months producing a gala dinner and stage show to be given in a grand marquee beside the ocean.

An hour before the party was scheduled to begin, a tempest arose and blew everything away. When Alain, in bedraggled jeans and T-shirt (he had been out on the beach trying to salvage the production), came to Elton's room to tell him the bad news, the singer's reaction was "Find me a piano!"

A piano was found and Elton did a whole show for all the invited guests: he saved the day.

Gifts and good turns go back and forth between these two friends. John Reid, who has been Elton's manager and close friend for sixteen years, reports that once when they were touring Europe they ran into some local difficulties with the aviation authorities, and Alain found a way to arrange for the tour to proceed smoothly. Alain treasures two mementoes of this episode—a little model airplane in gold made in St. Tropez and an Art Deco airplane made of wood (which stands in his office)—both presented to him by Elton John and John Reid in appreciation.

History and largesse are intertwined in the story of a palace of Trujillo, Spain, that was built in the thirteenth century, served as a Franciscan convent in the seventeenth century, was restored and occupied by the Vanderbilt Whitneys in the mid-twentieth century, and became the residence of internationally known interior designer Duarte Pinto Coelho on May 28, 1979.

Duarte Pinto is quietly eloquent on the subject: "I enjoy my beautiful home in Trujillo enormously; certainly it is the best gift of my life. It originally belonged to Mrs. Mary Lou Whitney, for whom I restored and decorated the vast seventeenth-century convent after her purchase. But Mrs. Whitney (with homes everywhere—and yet another in Spain, in Majorca) found she couldn't use it often enough to justify its beauty and importance, and she sold it to me for a song. It is now a focal point in my life and I cannot thank her enough for this generous act."

It is sometimes hard to tell largesse and magnanimity apart. Surely both impulses entered into the history of a memento with royal associations. Alice Keppel, the last of the royal mistresses, had presented to Edward VII a Fabergé cigarette case decorated with the striking design of a sensuously undulating serpent. Queen Alexandra not only summoned Mrs. Keppel to her dying husband's bedside but gave her back the cigarette case as a remembrance. In 1936 Mrs. Keppel presented it to Queen Mary for the royal collection.

Residence of Duarte Pinto Coelho in Trujillo, Spain

King Alexander of Yugoslavia was rarely seen without his Cartier cigarette case, an unusual piece wrought in yellow and red gold. After the King's tragic death by assassination in Marseilles in 1934, the case passed to his first cousin Prince Paul, who was Regent of Yugoslavia until 1941. This cherished possession was given by Prince Paul to his own son, the King's second cousin Prince Alexander, who had been a boy of ten, at school in England, when the assassination occurred. It means a great deal to him to have this Cartier piece that the King loved. "He was a man whom I loved more than anybody in this life, . . . and I have nothing else that belonged to him."

Prince Alexander worked for Cartier for a time, and while there he designed an engagement ring, which they executed, for his future wife, Princess Barbara of Liechtenstein. The ring is constantly worn; the King's cigarette case is a revered memento.

Above, Prince Alexander
and Princess Barbara of Yugoslavia

John Aspinall
to Sir James Goldsmith
and Edward Goldsmith

*The Aspinall Drum
and enamels*

Imagination, ingenuity, and generosity, backed by consummate craftsmanship, enabled John Aspinall to present his friends Sir James Goldsmith and Edward Goldsmith with unique gifts. The three friends represent diverse interests: John Aspinall owns a well-known West End gambling club and runs two zoos in Kent; Sir James Goldsmith, an Anglo-French industrial magnate, is the publisher of the French magazine *L'Express*; Edward Goldsmith, elder brother of Sir James, is publisher and editor of *The Ecologist* magazine.

John Aspinall's gift to Sir James is a collection of miniature enamels of, as he says, "all my wild animals,"

but this hardly does justice to the sphere of filigreed gold (incorporating the initials of the two friends, A and G) and its contents. Each animal is depicted on a semicircular segment framed in gold and set with gems, and the segments are attached to a spine so that they can be turned like book pages when not closed up in their golden case.

To Edward Goldsmith, John Aspinall gave a companion piece, the Aspinall Drum. It takes geography as its theme: on a blue enameled sea the continents are set in yellow gold. The places the friends visited together are marked with precious stones. These bibelots were the work of John Willmin, of N. Bloom & Son Ltd.

AFTERWORD

This is a book about memories. The best presents are units of time in three dimensions, perpetuating an occasion, a day, an instant. Each of the diverse remembrances that have found their way into these pages was, in its own way, a bid to outwit the transience of the moment.

People have undertaken this task in many and varied ways. If there is one strand binding together the flowers in this enormous bouquet of giving, it is the universal preference for a personal memento. The offerings cherished above all others seem to be those that hold a meaning beyond the worth of the gift or its substance. Some legendary beauties, for example, are seen to have chosen as their favorite remembrances, gifts that have little to do with the kind of tributes conventionally associated with the idolized.

Yet there is no question that the combination of wit, sensibility, and wealth makes possible ultimate expressions of generosity. A line from Euripides states the case, almost wistfully: "I care for riches, to make gifts to friends. . . ."

Remembrances that strike a special chord of delight are those that reveal an understanding of the aesthetic predilections of the recipient. A shared taste in art, objets d'art, and bibelots underlies many friendships and leads to the bestowal of presents that are as great a pleasure to find as to give. And how fortunate are the friends of collectors, whose special interests—whether pictures, plants, or postage stamps—give a clear, if inadvertent, signal.

Reading these pages, it is fascinating to be made aware so dramatically of the unlimited care and consideration, to say nothing of the imagination and ingenuity, that in many cases are put into the creation or devising of a remembrance. Such efforts, worthy of a work of art, often succeed in bringing about a memento that is indeed a work of art.

No novel, no sociological survey could be a better index to the infinite variety of human attitudes, human relations, and human priorities than a study of gift giving. Presents enshrine sentiment, and sentiment binds friend to friend, lover to lover, husband to wife, parent to child. Sentiment is rarely more highly valued than in gifts given to parents by their offspring. This does not hold only for gestures by the youngest members of the family; it holds for relationships between generations at all stages. Particularly in Europe, where a strong sense of family tradition exists, it is often the case that the younger generation takes special pleasure—and the initiative—in strengthening family ties.

Inscriptions and dedications are one of the unchanging ways in which keepsakes are given the hallmark of individuality. Many different approaches are adopted, each one adding the final fillip of particularity to the gift in question. In general a liking for privacy seems to surround the art of inscriptions, and they attach themselves to plaques on the back of framed photographs, the inside of boxes, the inside of rings, the bases of objects. But there are exceptions!

All the givers recorded in this volume are exemplary in one essential respect. They had each grasped a fundamental aspect of giving—that a present should always be chosen as an extra and not as a veiled necessity.

For the writer of the text of this work, the assembling of all these varied memories has been an enhancing experience. Wherever the theme of the art of giving led, into relations personal and professional, between young and old, between friends and strangers, it was all within a world—far removed from the dire headlines of the day—in which human nature went out of its way to be kind, generous, loving, and responsive. In this sense, it was a gift.

INDEX

WORKS CONSULTED

Dirk Bogarde, *Backdrop* (London: Penguin Books Ltd., 1980).

Dorothy Caruso, *Enrico Caruso: His Life and Death* (New York: Simon & Schuster, 1945).

Jean Cocteau Journals (London: Museum Press, 1957).

Joan Collins, *Past Imperfect: An Autobiography* (London: W.H. Allen, 1984).

Gilberte Gautier, *Cartier: The Legend* (London: Arlington, 1983).

Alec Guinness, *Blessings in Disguise* (London: Hamish Hamilton, 1985).

Jerry Hall, with Christopher Hemphill, *Jerry Hall's Tall Tales* (London: Elm Tree, 1985).

A.E. Hotchner, *Sophia, Living and Loving: Her Own Story* (New York: William Morrow, 1979).

Robert Lacey, *Aristocrats* (London: Hutchinson, 1983).

Cole Lesley, *The Life of Noël Coward* (London: Jonathan Cape, 1983).

Robert K. Massie, *Nicholas and Alexandra* (London: Gollancz, 1968).

Suzy Menkes, *The Royal Jewels* (London: Grafton, 1985).

Hans Nadelhoffer, *Cartier* (London: Thames & Hudson, 1984).

Graham Payn and Sheridan Morley, eds. *The Noël Coward Diaries* (London: Weidenfeld & Nicolson, 1982).

Liane de Pougy, *My Blue Notebooks* (London: André Deutsch, 1979).

Gertrude Stein, *The Autobiography of Alice B. Toklas* (London: Penguin Books Ltd., 1977).

Hugo Vickers, *Cecil Beaton* (London: Weidenfeld & Nicolson, 1985).

PHOTOGRAPH CREDITS

The publishers acknowledge with thanks the following sources of auxiliary photographs:

Stefan Alsen, 124 top; Lord Astor of Hever, 47 bottom; David Bailey, 48; Robyn Beeche, 194; Harry Benson, 58; Cartier–London, 85 top, 208; Mario Casilli, 135; Paul Cox, 41; Anthony Crickmay, 149; Gianni Dal Magro, 73; Studio Delorme, 170; Ecart, 198; Copyright reserved to Her Majesty Queen Elizabeth II, 207; Aldo Fallai, 202; Leonardo Ferragamo, 46 top; Rick Golt, 82 top; Halcyon Days, 46 bottom; Hever Castle Ltd., 47 top; David Hicks, 10; Horst, 121, 166; Jean Howard, 86, 184; Wolfgang Kuehn, 152; Ivan Kyncl, 22; Gemma Levine, 26; Duane Michals, 159; Derry Moore, 93; Movie Star News, 123, 138; Jacques Munch *France-Soir,* 102; National Trust Photographic Library, 79 bottom; J. de Nattes, 45 bottom; Julia Trevelyan Oman, C.B.E., 196; Terry O'Neil, 32; William S. Paley, 197; Norman Parkinson, 81; Antony Penrose, 49; Press Impact, 73; Rex Features, 110; John Rogers, 65; Eva Rubinstein, 108; Victor Skrebneski, 107; Sotheby's, 12 top; Alice Springs, 198; Star, 52; Robert Stein, 43; Steuben, 80 all; Sygma Photo News, 54; Daniel Teboul, 179; Tiffany & Co., 79 top; Wartski, 113; Albert Watson, 43; Janet Young, 211.